GUERRILLA DEAL-MAKING

Critical acclaim for

GUERRILLA
DEAL-MAKING

"Maximize your profits. Minimize your losses. Win more often. Lose less often." Yeah, I've heard all this before too. But *Guerrilla Deal-Making* is different—it's a comprehensive reference book that tells you when to be assertive, when to go on the defense, when to cooperate, and how to handle dirty tricks. I love it! You will, too!

—**Tony Alessandra**, author of *The Platinum Rule* and *Charisma* and Hall-of-Fame Keynote Speaker

What a fabulous book this is! We all need to negotiate at some stage. Most of us fail to prepare enough—we often fail to research the person we are going to negotiate with and sadly, in the dog-eat-dog business world, we often go into negotiations with a win/lose attitude. We go in to win, but because we haven't researched or planned or understood the other party, we end up losing. Even if you are Donald Trump or Mao Tse-Tung. Absolutely the best book I've ever read on negotiating!

—**Ann Andrews**, Managing Director, The Corporate Toolbox (Auckland, New Zealand)

For over 30 years I've studied business deal-making. and this is the first new approach to the topic that I've seen in decades! You will become a better deal-maker by reading this book. Get it now before you make another flawed deal without even realizing it.

—**Jim Cathcart**, author of *Relationship Selling*

Don Hendon tackles the problem of reading a customer's mind from a unique perspective. He categorizes every possible tactic that you might encounter during a business negotiation. But he does more than that—he gives you the upper hand by telling you the recommended counter-move to each tactic. It's almost unfair, because you're going to cream your competition with this information.

—**Tim Van Milligan**, President of www.customersecrets.com

Guerrilla Deal Making has to be the best blend of a self-help book and business book I've ever seen. It's full of practical wisdom. I keep referring to it over and over. I know you will too—and that's a good thing! In fact, it's absolutely incredible! I know it will profoundly change your life by making you considerably more successful.

—**David Hancock**, Publisher, Morgan James

Wow! *Guerrilla Deal-Making* has more practical, useful ideas on closing the deal than any book I've ever seen. The first chapter alone, Donald Trump vs. Mao Tse-Tung at the Negotiating Table, blew me away with the powerful, creative ideas, and the engaging writing style. This is a *must-read* for serious negotiators!

—**Jim Hennig**, author of *How to Say It: Negotiating to Win*
and past President of National Speakers Association

Don Hendon will take you inside the mind of the most famous guerrilla of all time—Mao Tse-Tung—in a make-believe, fascinating, hilarious, gripping, and believable negotiation with Donald Trump. You will learn how a real guerrilla succeeds in a give-and-take with a real capitalist. The entire book is original, brilliant, and powerful!

—**Steve Savage**, author of *Guerrilla Business Secrets*

I'm a darned good negotiator—I've made a lot of money making deals. But the ideas I got here in this book are so unique and powerful, I tried some of them out right away. And guess what? I made a lot more money than I could have made using my usual techniques.

—**Doug Nielsen**, author of *Take Life by the Helm:
Proven Strategies for Gaining Control*

If you're a successful guerrilla or hoping to become one, the art of making a good deal is your most important weapon. Whether negotiating with vendors, clients, and even employees, nothing will increase your bottom line better than how well you cut the deal. Donald Hendon's *Guerrilla Deal-Making* is packed with creative one-up deal making approaches that, believe me, you've never considered. It's not just *must-read*—it's *must-learning*.

—**Bob Kaden**, author of *Guerrilla Marketing Research* and President of The Kaden Company

With over two lifetimes of research and practice, Jay Conrad Levinson and Donald Hendon have cracked the code to sealing the deal. *Guerrilla Deal-Making* will give you a powerful new way of thinking, how to avoid costly mistakes and give you the weapons you need to finish the deal.

—**Kurt Mortensen**, author of *Persuasion IQ*, *Maximum Influence*, and *The Laws of Charisma*

Guerrilla Deal-Making will help you win in business through one of the most critical skills you can cultivate: effective negotiating. Jay Conrad Levinson, the father of Guerrilla Marketing, and Donald Wayne Hendon, the cross-cultural negotiations expert, have teamed up to bring you an instant business classic. There isn't a better bottom-line payoff you can get from a single business skill than this one.

—**Stuart Burkow**, president of www.kingofprofits.com and small business advocate

Hundreds of practical, powerful, negotiating tactics to use and defend against…one of the best negotiating books in the past 20 years. A *must-read*.

—**Steven Babitsky**, author of *Never Lose Again* and President of SEAK Inc.

Whether, like me, you're intrigued by tales of Mao and Donald Trump, or you just want to benefit from the negotiation savvy of these prolific authors, *Guerrilla Deal-Making* is one book you can't afford to miss.

—**Ed Brodow**, author of *Negotiation Boot Camp*

Unfortunately, most businesses haven't a clue about how to negotiate a win/win conclusion across global cultural frontiers. Imperative in a truly globalized world. Don and Jay have produced an essential book for today's manager—required reading for staying in business.

—**Michael Hick**, author, *Global Deals—Marketing and Managing Across Cultural Frontiers*

Who wouldn't want to become the ultimate guerilla when it comes down to closing the deal ... any deal? Master deal-maker Don Hendon has created the only guidebook you need today—whether it's huge or small, his *Guerrilla Deal-Making* becomes a *must-have*.

—**Judith Briles**, author of *The Confidence Factor*

Do you sometimes play Poker with your negotiating when you should be playing Chess, or vice versa? *Guerrilla Deal-Making* will improve your deal-making skills pronto. It revives many classic sales strategies and reveals many all-new ones for every deal situation. I suggest you read it twice, and then keep it on your nightstand. A *must-read* for every serious sales pro.

—**Rob Northrup**, President of Advanced Extrusion Solutions

Jay and Don's book will profoundly affect your life—not only will it help you become a better buyer or seller, it will improve your relationship with the people that mean the most to you—your family. It's really that powerful! A gold mine of useful information.

—**Rick Frishman**, founder of Planned TV Arts

Jay Conrad Levinson and Donald Wayne Hendon bring unique strengths to this outstanding book. Jay's entrepreneurial and marketing wisdom combined with Don's remarkable deal-making experience around the world enable them to help all small businesses make win-win deals in the great Guerrilla Marketing tradition. A pleasure to read, this handy, right-on-the-money guide will enable you to make the most of any negotiation.

—**Michael Larsen**, author of *Guerrilla Marketing for Writers*

All of us want to get others to do what we want them to do. Sellers want higher prices. Buyers want lower prices. Parents want kids to pick up their clothes. We all want to be winners when we flirt. We all want to talk our way out of speeding tickets. This is the one and only book I've ever read that tells me how to do all these things. It's worked wonders for me, and it will for you, too!

—**Joe Vitale**, author of *The Attractor Factor*

Want something from somebody else? You could steal it. That's not recommended. Instead, use the negotiating strategies and techniques you'll absorb from this book. It's loaded with specific, practical, and easy-to-use proven ways to turn you into a power negotiator. And… it's written in a reader friendly and entertaining style that makes it a fun read.

—**David Graska**, President, David Graska Business Development

This book will definitely change your attitude about negotiations. Whether you are an expert or an ordinary Joe, it will change your life forever.

—**Krassimir Petrov**, Professor, St. Joseph's University, Macau

Make "Getting to New Levels" more than a cliché. How? By following the advice you'll get here from two masters of the art of deal-making. It's not your father's deal-making. Whatever you learn here, you can apply immediately. Do yourself a guerrilla favor and buy the book, read the book, and implement before your competition does. See you at the top!!

—**Al Lautenslager**, author of *Guerrilla Marketing in 30 Days* and president of Market for Profits

The next must-read for any disciple of Guerrilla Marketing.

—**Orvel Ray Wilson**, author of *Guerrilla Retailing*

Wow, all I can say after reading *Guerrilla Deal-Making* is, I want to go out and make some deals happen. Don has a clever way of motivating the reader to action, and if you are a person who thinks big and makes big decisions, then this is the book to pick up and read!

—**Grant Hicks**, President of www.FinancialAdvisorMarketing.com and author of *Guerrilla Marketing for Financial Advisors*

There's no need to buy dozens of books on negotiating. Buy this one! It offers astounding strategies that you can use immediately! The best part

about this book is it's applicable to readers world-wide! Don't delay...
buy it today!

—**Michael Aun**, author of *It's the Customer, Stupid!*
and member of Speakers Hall of Fame

If you want to want to influence others, this book shows you how!
Using the 100 powerful weapons in this book will make you the big
winner. And if others use them against you, there are more than 400
counter-punches to choose from. I loved reading it, and you will, too!

—**Aaron Young**, CEO of Laughlin Associates

Get this book. Read and learn from the different negotiating styles
of Donald Trump and many successful negotiators. Mao Tse-Tung, too.
Then, before negotiating any serious deal, pull the book off the shelf and
read the 20 Do's and 20 Don'ts of Concession-Making. If there were
nothing else in this book, this would be more than worth the price—but
those two checklists are only the beginning of the treasures within.

—**Shel Horowitz**, author of *Guerrilla Marketing Goes Green*,
consultant, and President of www.GreenandProfitable.com

This book is both for winners and losers. Winners will keep on
winning when they use the 100 powerful tactics in Jay and Don's
book. And when losers use them, they'll quickly become winners. Just
imagine—a world full of winners! What an exciting, wonderful place
that would be!

—**Tom Antion**, President of Internet Marketing
Training Center of Virginia

I wish I had read this book years ago. It would have saved me from
making a lot of mistakes. All of us learn the tricks of the trade by trial
and error and by observation. Reading Jay and Don's book will shorten
that process for you. You'll enter the winner's circle much, much sooner.

—**James Dillehay**, author of *Guerrilla Multilevel Marketing*

Enter the winner's circle and stay there! How? By following the
advice you'll get here from two masters of the art of deal-making. You
can apply their techniques immediately. I strongly urge you to use these

easy-to-understand, practical tactics as soon as possible—before your competitors do!

—**Marcella Vonn Harting**, PhD, author of
Guerrilla Multilevel Marketing

How can you beat the "Big Boys" when they play dirty during negotiations? By learning before you start what those techniques are and how to counterattack. Jay and Don give you an inside expert's view of the secret tricks and tactics of power negotiators and what to do when you come face-to-face with them.

—**Linda Swindling**, author of *Get What You Want*

Guerilla Deal-Making is a *must-read* for everybody who has the desire to reach great heights with their product or service. This insightful book clarifies and shares with you how to make it all happen. I have read all of the *Guerilla Marketing* books and have used many of the ideas successfully. This one is the very best!

—**Carol Stanley**, author of *For Kids 59.99 and Over*

Having the pleasure of meeting both of the authors and learning first-hand the value each brings to this book, your purchase is well justified because every chapter is chock-full of the most relevant content published to date. This book will be an invaluable asset to anyone possessing its knowledge.

—**Brian Latta**, CEO of Trader Development—
The International Association of Traders, Inc.

Instructive and practical analysis of negotiating tactics presented in an imaginative and entertaining way. Learn the tricks for getting a better deal. Written in an easy, engaging style. Almost like attending a seminar with a consummate lecturer. A great read.

—**Hernan Contreras**, international entrepreneur

This book will be for the ages. A winning approach in dealing with modern day competition. A powerful book that will revolutionize your thinking and improve your profits and market share. A *must-read*.

—**Fermin Castillo**, Professor of Strategic Management, University of Jazeera, Dubai, United Arab Emirates

Don's work is by far and away the best I have ever seen and used. His grasp and understanding of negotiations and the human dynamics of persuasion is superb. Not only can you make money with this book, you can change your life. A masterpiece!

—**Linc Miller**, Sandler Training

GUERRILLA DEAL-MAKING

How to Put the Big Dog on Your Leash and Keep Him There

JAY CONRAD LEVINSON
& DONALD WAYNE HENDON

GUERRILLA MARKETING PRESS
an imprint of Morgan James Publishing
NEW YORK

GUERRILLA DEAL-MAKING
How to Put the Big Dog on Your Leash and Keep Him There

ISBN 978-1-61448-244-4 Paperback
ISBN 978-1-61448-245-1 eBook
Library of Congress Control Number: 2012932343

GUERRILLA MARKETING PRESS
an imprint of
Morgan James Publishing
The Entrepreneurial Publisher
5 Penn Plaza, 23rd Floor,
New York City, New York 10001
(212) 655-5470 office • (516) 908-4496 fax
www.MorganJamesPublishing.com

Cover Design by:
Rachel Lopez
www.r2cdesign.com

Interior Design by:
Bonnie Bushman
bonnie@caboodlegraphics.com

In an effort to support local communities, raise awareness and funds, Morgan James Publishing donates a percentage of all book sales for the life of each book to Habitat for Humanity Peninsula and Greater Williamsburg.

Get involved today, visit
www.MorganJamesBuilds.com.

DEDICATION

Jay dedicates this book to his four-year old granddaughter, Cali Adkins, who is the best deal-maker he knows.

Don dedicates this book to his sweet and wonderful wife, Eda, the love of his life, the wind beneath his wings.

TABLE OF CONTENTS

Chapter 3 tells you what's really going on inside the mind of the big dog—the powerful opponent guerrillas face in the deal-making process. After you read this chapter, you'll know how to take advantage of his Big I, Little You attitude. You'll learn many subtle guerrilla tricks to win him over to your side.

Chapter 4 gives you the complete—and improved—list of Don Hendon's 365 deal-making tactical Weapons contained in his 365 Powerful Ways to Influence book. The 100 most powerful techniques are in bold-face type, so they stand out. We've also included Mao Tse-Tung's 22 favorite Guerrilla Weapons.

In Chapter 16, you'll learn how to tell what's going on in the minds of both big dogs and other guerrillas without them even suspecting that you *know. How to tell if they're lying or if they're trying to dominate you. What their touches mean. Get more clues from how they set up their office. And best of all, you'll also learn how to manipulate them with your own body language. If you do it correctly, they probably won't suspect a thing.*

Chapter 17 is all about how to make concessions the right way—and how to make the other guy give you more concessions than he really wants to.

INTRODUCTION

BY JAY CONRAD LEVINSON

You give a great deal of thought to your product, service or company. You've packaged it properly. Your website is a winner. Your marketing is bang on target. Your price is ideal for your market and your profitability. Your positioning couldn't be better. And your management team is gold medal all the way. Your ideal client calls you on the phone and wants to discuss a huge purchase they want to make from you.

You meet…and everything is downhill from there. You make several unnecessary concessions to your customer, agree on a schedule that will tax your people more severely than ever—and you hardly make any profit from the whole deal.

How could that happen? It happens every day and everywhere because most people have only the faintest notion on how to make the best possible deal. Faced with a deal-maker who has far more savvy about making a deal, you become a leaning tower of Jell-O and miss out on profits due not to how smart you *aren't*, but due to your inexperience at making a remarkably wise deal every single time.

That won't happen to you when you've finished this book. Don Hendon, the lead dude on this project, is to deal-making what Babe Ruth was to baseball. A guerrilla through and through for five decades, Don points out the most important tips for starting out as a sure winner along with the most painful mistakes you can make during the exquisite process of making a deal.

It's not exquisite to those on the short end of the deal. It *is* exquisite to guerrillas who know the intricacies of deal-making and Don's 365 powerful *Guerrilla Navigating Weapons.* They are both unquestionably fair and impressively profitable.

Those 365 Weapons, plus the best that we have mined from Don's fascinating stories of negotiating, clue you in on deal-making as guerrillas practice it around the world. Those stories will grant to you the power to win and win big-time. Americans, sad to say, aren't entirely clued in on insights, but they will be after they've devoured this book of essential business wisdom.

If you've ever pondered how to bring the big dog down to the size of a puppy, you'll ponder no more.

Don and I have but two things to ask of you:

1. Please don't sit across the table from us at the negotiating table after you've read this.
2. Read this cover to cover before those you will deal with read it.

We're confident this book will help you come out on top in every negotiation and add to your knowledge in many ways beyond business.

—*Jay Conrad Levinson*
DeBary, Florida

PART ONE

BIG DOGS AND GUERRILLAS—AN INTRODUCTION TO GUERRILLA DEAL-MAKING

CHAPTER 1

DONALD TRUMP VS. MAO TSE-TUNG AT THE NEGOTIATING TABLE

onald Trump and Mao Tse-Tung want to make a deal. Just imagine! Today's capitalist big-shot and the guerrilla warfare expert of the middle 20th century! Use your imagination. Here's how this "fractured fairy tale" *could* have happened:

Trump Sends a Feeler to Mao

One of Donald Trump's top executives contacted one of Mao's closest friends and told him that Trump wants to build a casino-hotel in Shanghai that would be larger than any of the casino-hotels in Vegas and Macau—a tribute to Trump's huge ego. One of Mao's biggest hobbies is gambling, and he has already set up several small private casinos in Beijing for him and his close friends to use. Mao likes the money Trump's executive is talking about, but he knows he can get a lot more from him. And he really wants to get the best of that obnoxious capitalist, who likes to call himself "The Donald." Mao has said for years that The Donald is Donald Duck, and so he started calling Trump "The Haircut." Likewise, Trump's oversized ego makes him think that Mao is nothing more than a naïve country boy who is no match for Trump. "I'll have fun beating him to a pulp."

3

Question 1. Do you see trouble ahead? What dumb mistakes are these two guys making? We'll give you the answer at the end of this chapter.

At first, Mao thought it was strange that The Haircut was interested in Shanghai and not Macau, the former Portuguese colony, which became a part of China in 1999. Macau's casino industry had grown rapidly in recent years. Three giants in the Vegas casino industry, all multi-billionaires, had built huge casino-hotels in Macau in the last ten years. Steve Wynn, who owns Wynn's and Encore. Kirk Kerkorian, big stockholder in MGM Resorts International, which owns many hotels, including the Bellagio, MGM Grand, Luxor, and Monte Carlo. And Sheldon Adelson, whose Las Vegas Sands Corporation owns the Venetian and Palazzo. Adelson also owns the huge Marina Bay Sands in Singapore—the government there gave him a monopoly for ten years.

All of a sudden, Mao had an Aha! moment. "Trump is in a pissing contest with Adelson, Wynn, and Kerkorian. He wants to get into mainland China so he can build its biggest casino-hotel—one that would put the three other guys' casino-hotels in Macau to shame!" Then, Mao thought, "It would be fun to get into a pissing contest with that egotistical maniac, Donald Trump. I'll win, for sure. There's no way in hell I would lose to The Haircut in my own country. He's going to build here, and I'm not going to build anything in the U.S. Here, I control all the shots. There, The Haircut and his cronies in the U.S. government control things. I think I'll see what Trump has to offer."

Question 2. Mao is now making what three dumb mistakes?

So after getting some initial feelers from Trump's flunkies, he decided to research The Haircut—his life, his past dealings. He figured Trump, like all capitalists, would be an easy mark.

Question 3. This question is not about dumb mistakes. Instead, we are asking you something else. What Deal-Making Weapon is Mao is using now? (A complete list of Don's 365 Deal-Making Weapons and Don's list of the 22 strongest of Mao's Guerrilla Warfare Weapons are in Chapter Four.)

Question 4: And what dumb mistake is Mao making now?

Mao Thinks About It—Hard

Mao got Chinese translations of a couple of books which told everybody who read them what The Haircut's favorite negotiating weapons are—the ones he uses the most. Both were written by Trump's associates. One by Schwartz, the other by Ross. "What an idiot Trump is," Mao thought. "I would never reveal my favorite weapons to anybody. Knowledge is power. The more I know, the more powerful I am. The less the other person knows, the less powerful he is."

Question 5. What Weapon is Mao thinking about now?

"I'll never be as stupid as The Haircut is—he's already made an important concession to me before we even began to negotiate. He gave me a lot of important knowledge about himself without getting anything from me in return. I wonder why he doesn't know what we Chinese have always known—never give a concession without getting something in return."

Question 6. What Weapon is Mao thinking about now?

Mao thought back to the old days of the 1930s and 1940s when he had spies in Chiang-Kai-Shek's army. "They fed Chiang wrong information about me and told me what he was going to do next. That's the main reason I defeated him." Mao had no contacts in Trump's organization, so he decided to let himself be interviewed by the western news media. He knew they would jump at a chance to interview him, and he was sure that The Haircut would read what the media said.

Question 7. Mao is now using what two Weapons?

Mao Takes Action

So the next day, Mao gave one of his few interviews to CCTV, the number one Chinese cable news channel in the world. He knew CCTV would translate his words into English. He didn't want to give a newspaper interview, because he didn't want The Haircut to *read* his words—he wanted Trump to only *hear* his words. He figured Haircut Guy would remember words on paper, but would forget many words he heard on TV.

Question 8. What dumb mistake is Mao making now?

Here are the most important things he said in the interview:

"I have always disliked capitalism. Over the years, though, I learned that I can take advantage of the greed all capitalists have. I understand several entrepreneurs in the United States are interested in opening up Las Vegas-style casinos in our largest city, Shanghai. Many people in Shanghai already travel to Macau, around 800 miles away, a three-hour airplane trip. And all they do there is spend the weekend gambling. This was bad a few years ago, because Macau wasn't even part of China. But Macau is part of China today, so that makes it acceptable to me. But traveling so far away from their cities just to gamble is wasteful. I would like Shanghai residents to stay in Shanghai and have the Macau and Las Vegas experience in their own city. So I'm open to the idea of building the world's biggest casino-hotel in Shanghai. I invite inquiries from owners of big casinos in Vegas—people like Sheldon Adelson, Kirk Kerkorian, and Steve Wynn. And maybe even Donald Trump."

Question 9. Mao is making another dumb mistake. What is it?

When Trump heard the news, he got a copy of the English translation of Mao's interview. Trump ordered his most trusted executives to set up a meeting with Mao himself. Trump wanted to meet Mao in Las Vegas at the Trump International Hotel, a block away from the Las Vegas Strip. 64 stories tall, it was opened in 2008. Trump was planning to build a second 64-story tower right next door. Trump considered this hotel to be the crowning jewel in all of the Trump empire—bigger and more luxurious than his three casino-hotels in Atlantic City, New Jersey. And he thought Mao would be impressed by the fact that he was doubling its size. He wanted to show off by taking Mao around the construction site himself.

In the meantime, Mao turned down meetings with Adelson, Kerkorian, and Wynn. They already had hotel-casinos in China—in Macau. He wasn't after more money from them. He not only wanted to win a pissing contest with the biggest capitalistic ego in the world, Donald Trump, he also wanted to humiliate The Haircut and bring him down to earth.

Question 10. What Weapon is Mao using now?

And there was a lot of icing on the cake. Mao loved the idea of visiting fabulous Las Vegas. He thought to himself, "I've heard about this city for many years. It's very famous. There are many more casinos there than there are in Macau. I'd like to see for myself what it's all about. Maybe I can duplicate some of its best features in Shanghai."

Question 11. What dumb mistake is Mao making now?

So Mao agreed to the meeting in Las Vegas. Trump reserved the presidential suite at the top of his Trump International Hotel. And threw in 20 more floors of rooms for Mao's entourage.

Mao Comes to Sin City

When Mao arrived at McCarran Airport in Vegas, Trump himself met him and whisked him away in his private helicopter. After they landed on the top of Trump's hotel, Mao told The Haircut he wanted to see the hotel's casino area before he saw his suite. Mao was shocked to find out that the Trump

Hotel did not have a casino. Haircut Guy explained that several of the more expensive hotels on the Strip had no casinos—not just Trump's hotel but also the Ritz-Carlton, Four Seasons, J W Marriott, Turnberry Towers, and others. Mao didn't like that explanation—he thought Trump was lying to him. So he asked his aides to visit those four hotels. Sure enough, all were on the strip, all were five-star caliber (except for Turnberry), and none of them had casinos.

Mao relaxed for the next few days. Got rid of his jet lag. Played a little poker. He didn't leave Trump's hotel except for a couple of helicopter trips which gave him a good view of Vegas and the Strip. One afternoon, he took a helicopter trip to the famous Grand Canyon.

Before he left on his trip to the U.S., one of his aides had given him Donald Wayne Hendon's book, *365 Powerful Ways to Influence* (Pelican, 2010), to read. His aide told him this was the best negotiating book he had ever seen. Mao read it before he left for Vegas, and he was very impressed. During the three days he was relaxing in Vegas, waiting for the negotiating sessions with The Haircut to begin, he looked over Trump's 1988 book, *Trump: The Art of the Deal*, really written by one of Trump's most trusted employees, Tony Schwartz. That book listed The Haircut's favorite 11 deal-making weapons. Because of Trump's huge ego, it even included 42 pictures—baby pictures, pictures of Trump buildings, and other personal stuff. Mao's aides told him it wasn't a very good book, but it wasn't as bad as *Trump-Style Negotiation*, written in 2006 by another Trump employee, George Ross.

Mao said to one of the members of his entourage, "Trump seems to have 11 favorite Negotiating Weapons, according to this book. All of them sound similar to many of Donald Hendon's 365 Negotiating Weapons. Tell me which weapons Dr. Hendon talks about correspond to Schwartz's 11 weapons. That will help me when I negotiate with Trump." His aide gave him a summary of this information on five sheets of paper, and Mao studied these sheets during those three days. He wasn't surprised that the list of Trump's favorite 11 weapons didn't include any tactical weapons that Chinese people really use a lot. Such as Hendon's *Tuangou / Swarming Ambush / Flash Mobs* (Assertive Weapon 58), where many people overpower a single person. And *A Chinese favorite—The Rule of Three* (Assertive Weapon 25), where you say no at least three times before finally saying yes.

Mao memorized Trump's favorite 11 negotiating weapons and came up with several counter-punches for each one. Trump's 11 weapons and Don Hendon's corresponding tactical Weapons are:

Donald Trump's favorite 11 negotiating weapons	Name and number of Don Hendon's corresponding Deal-Making Weapons
1. Contain the costs	Intimidate him by your money (Assertive 84)
2. Deliver the goods	Hey, let's look at the record (Assertive 104). Complete honesty—reveal your bottom line (Cooperative 8)
3. Enhance your location	Negotiate where you have the most power—your place (Assertive 57)
4. Fight back	Don't lose your momentum—don't give in to unreasonable demands (Defensive 89)
5. Get the word out—be outrageous	Act egotistical—I'm the greatest! (Assertive 39). The bandwagon effect—lead a parade (Assertive 40). Get good publicity from news media (Defensive 79)
6. Have fun	Calm down and lighten up (Preparation 12)
7. Know your market	Know your enemy and know yourself—Knowledge is power (Assertive 32)
8. Maximize your options	The squeaky wheel—flexible persistence (Assertive 102). Be sure—use off-setting bets (Assertive 121). Remind TOS of his competition—real or imaginary (Defensive 4). Important note: TOS stands for *the other side*
9. Protect your downside, and the upside will take care of itself	Become hard to convince (Preparation 7)
10. Think big	Size matters—the big pot (Assertive 48)
11. Use your leverage	For sellers: Make buyers pursue you for a change (Assertive 20)

Mao's aide told him The Haircut would also use Don's Assertive Weapon 95 against Mao and that Mao should use this same weapon on Trump. It's called *Intimidate the other side if you're a celebrity.*

The Guerrilla Comes to The Haircut's Office

Eventually, Mao and Trump met in Trump's office. Mao thought he was prepared. He remembered Don Hendon's 13 tactical Weapons (Assertive 83-95) used to intimidate TOS. (*Important note*: Throughout your book, TOS stands for *the other side*, or *the other person*. We will remind you about this at the beginning of each chapter.) Mao wondered which ones The Haircut would use on him:

Intimidate me by his height. Trump is 6 foot 2 inches. I am tall by Chinese standards, but The Haircut is a lot taller than me. He'll probably try and use this on me.

By his money. He's already tried to impress me with his wealth. I'm glad he thinks he can afford to give it away—I'll take as much of it as I can. The negotiating is what's fun, but money is how you keep score.

By acting like Santa Claus. He's already used that on me—showing me he can afford to give money away. Well, let him do it some more.

By using lawful, legitimate power. He's not a policeman.

By his charisma. With his big ego, he thinks he's charismatic, but that's a big blind spot. I see through him.

By rewarding me or punishing me. I have that power, he doesn't. He wants to build a casino-hotel in Shanghai. I don't want anything from him but his money.

By using big words. We speak through interpreters, so I don't pay attention to his vocabulary—just to his body language.

By his title and status. He's chairman of the board of his company, but that doesn't impress me.

By his credentials. He probably has a university degree, but so what!

By his occupation. I wonder what he thinks his occupation is.

By being untouchable. He thinks his connections make him invulnerable. But I'm the one with this power. I don't need any connections. I am supreme ruler of China.

By being a celebrity. He's well-known, but I'm better-known than he is, all around the world.

By his expertise or by bringing an expert with him. He'll probably try to impress me by showing me how much he knows about the casino-hotel business. But his three Atlantic City casino-hotels went bankrupt.

So Mao figured Trump would try to intimidate him by height. But Mao wasn't prepared for what he saw when he walked into Trump's office for the first time. Mao was shocked and awed when he walked into The Haircut's average-size office. Several huge oil paintings of Trump. His custom-made desk dominated the place. Polished teak. At least 15 feet wide, maybe five feet from Trump's edge to Mao's edge. Absolutely nothing on it—not one piece of paper. The world's biggest and cleanest desk! Trump reached into the pocket of his coat for a pad of paper and a gold ball-point pen so he could take notes.

Question 12. What Weapon is Trump using now?

After the initial shock wore off, Mao noticed several things. Sure enough, Trump's chair was much higher than Mao's chair—The Haircut used intimidation by height. The hot and bright Las Vegas sun was in Mao's face. The glare was awful. He and Trump were face-to-face, a confrontational position. Not in the friendlier position of sitting diagonally across from each other at one of the corners. And Mao's chair seemed to wobble a little bit.

Question 13. Trump is now using what four Dirty Tricks?

Mao Leaves Suddenly

A lot of things were racing through Mao's mind in those first five minutes. He thought about the days when he fought and beat the much stronger Chiang Kai-Shek who then ruled China. "I was a true guerrilla in those days. I followed guerrilla warfare principles. I even wrote them down in my own book, *Yu Chi Chan*. I controlled the shots then. Why am I allowing The Haircut to control the shots here? I think I should leave now and go back to Beijing. Trump's ego is ruling him—he wants to build his casino-hotel in Shanghai very much. A lot more than I want to humiliate him by taking as much money as I can from him, letting him build his casino-hotel in Beijing, and then take it away from him by passing a law. I can't use my guerrilla warfare weapons here in Las Vegas. I can use them back in Beijing."

And so Mao decided to gamble by walking out right away. He told The Haircut, "I don't want to negotiate with you here. Come to Beijing. We'll negotiate there." Trump's jaw dropped when Mao got up and quickly left the room with his translator and entourage, without giving a reason—and before Trump had time to object.

Are You a Big Dog or a Guerrilla at Heart?

This is where the *real story* begins. Our book—now *your* book—is about guerrilla deal-making. How the little dog can beat the big dog by refusing to play by the big dog's rules. But before we begin the *real story*, ask yourself this important question: Who were you rooting for—Mao or Trump? Hoping Mao would win doesn't necessarily make you a guerrilla at heart, and hoping Trump would win doesn't necessarily mean you're a big dog at heart. Here's how to *really* tell:

Big Dog Dealmaker at Heart	Factor	Guerrilla Dealmaker at Heart
This deal is complicated and hard to understand	Overall attitude	I can—and will—control the complexity of the deal
As big as possible	Budgets	Focus on energy, imagination, and investment of time, not on size
By offering allied products and services	Diversification—how to do it	By offering products and services that create synergy with my present line
Linear growth, by adding new customers	Growth—how to do it	Use service and follow-up to create more and larger deals from my present customers and by getting referrals from them

Concentrate on counting monthly receipts	Number-crunching	Count number of relationships made each month—the more relationships, the more receipts in the future
Experience plus judgment, lots of guesswork	Orientation	Psychology—what's in my customer's mind
Executives in both large and small businesses, whose companies almost always bankroll their ideas	Size of business	Most executives in small businesses, who dream big but have small bankrolls
Sales	Success—measuring it	Profits
It's too complicated, expensive, limited. So go with traditional methods	Technology—view on using it	It's simple to use, reasonably priced, and limitless in potential
Just a few costly ones	Weapons—kinds of weapons	Use many weapons, especially those which cost you nothing
Stay simple—use the one that always works the best	Weapons—number of weapons	Get synergy by using a combination of weapons

Be honest with yourself. If you're a big dog at heart, you've got a lot to learn. If you're a guerrilla at heart, your book will help you win more, not only from big dogs but from other guerrillas. And as you go through your book, always remember this—deal-making is not just a contest. *Successful* deal-making is all about collaboration and mutual problem-solving.

An Offer Too Good to Refuse

Before we end this chapter, let us make you an offer you can't refuse. After you finish reading your book, write a Fractured Fairy Tale about what happened *after* Donald Trump travels to Beijing to continue negotiating with Mao Tse-Tung. Please send it to Don at **www.GuerrillaDon.com**. Jay and Don will pick the best fairy tale and reward the writer with $1,000. The winner will also be invited to attend Jay's three-day Guerrilla Boot Camp, free of charge. Your fairy tale will appear in our next book.

What the Rest of Your Book Is About

Both of us are Americans who have made deals with executives all over the world. Don has negotiated deals on behalf of companies on six continents. He has given several thousand seminars on deal-making. Guerrillas and big dogs from more than 60 countries have attended his programs and learned his 365 negotiating Weapons. He knows which Weapons most people use over and over again—and which Weapons most people usually avoid. He knows which Weapons work and which ones don't work. And he knows which nationalities are good at deal-making and which nationalities are terrible.

Are Americans good or terrible? Here's a hint: Foreigners love to deal with Americans. Why? Because their experience has shown them that Americans are notoriously bad deal-makers—not very good at getting what they want from foreigners and from each other. Here's why foreigners have a low opinion of American negotiators: They think Americans have a big dog mentality. That's probably true. In general, we Americans think our nation is number one in almost everything, even in areas where we don't excel. Overseas, we let everybody know "We're the greatest," which is Assertive Weapon 39 in Don's book, *365 Powerful Ways to Influence*.

And so Chapter Two gives you the 18 reasons why Americans are sub-par at deal-making. It also tells you how to avoid the dumb mistakes and assumptions that make Americans get a lot less than they could when they try to close a deal.

Chapter Three tells you what's going on inside the mind of the big dog. The powerful opponent guerrillas face in the deal-making process. After you read this chapter, you'll know how to take advantage of his *Big I, Little You* attitude. You'll learn many subtle guerrilla tricks to win him over to your side.

Chapter Four gives you a complete list of Don Hendon's 365 deal-making tactical Weapons contained in his book, *365 Powerful Ways to Influence*. The 100 most powerful techniques are in bold-face type, so they stand out. We've also included Mao's 22 favorite Guerrilla Weapons.

Chapters Five, Six, Seven, Eight, and Nine thoroughly discuss the 50 most powerful Weapons that most people *don't* use very often. They are ideally suited for guerrillas. Use them to surprise people when you make deals with them. Chapters 10, 11, 12, 13, 14, and 15 contain the 50 most powerful Weapons that are *over-used* by people all over the world. You'll see them used against you often.

In Chapters 5-15, you'll find over 400 counter-punches to use against these 100 tactical Weapons which your opponents won't expect. When you use them, you'll put these big dogs and other guerrillas off-balance. Taking advantage of their rhythm when they're unsettled will help you win the deal.

Chapter 16 gives you insights into body language. You'll learn how to tell what's going on in the minds of both big dogs and guerrillas without them knowing that you know. And you'll also learn how to manipulate them with *your own* body language. If you do it correctly, they probably won't suspect a thing. (Don's next book is *Guerrilla Body Language*. Watch for it.)

Chapter 17 is a very important part of guerrilla deal-making. It's all about how to make concessions the right way—and how to make the other guy give you more concessions than he really wants to.

Chapter 18 shows you how to become so skilled at guerrilla deal-making, you make the right move at the right time—almost automatically. You'll also learn how to use Jay's 54 Golden Rules for Guerrilla Marketing Excellence to win big and win more often. This chapter really puts you in the guerrilla mood, preparing you for your incredible journey to higher profits. About the Authors is at the end of the chapter.

This is going to be an enjoyable—and very practical—journey. Let's get started. On your mark, get set, go!

Answers to 13 Questions in This Chapter

Question 1. Do you see trouble ahead? What dumb mistakes are these two guys making?

Answer: Both men are underestimating their rivals.

Note: Please go to **www.GuerrillaDon.com** to get information about Don's comprehensive list of 100 smart moves and 100 dumb mistakes in deal-making. They will be in his forthcoming book, *Deal-Makers and Deal-Breakers: 100 Smart Moves and 100 Dumb Mistakes*.

Question 2. Mao is now making what three dumb mistakes?

Answer:

1. Under-estimating his rival again.
2. Building in China (Mao's country), but negotiating in the US (Trump's country). Mao knew the casino-hotel would be built in China, but he made the wrong assumption that the negotiation would happen in China as well. He ignored Don's Defensive Weapon 23 in Chapter Four, Assumptions—use them wisely. All of Don's 365 Weapons are in Chapter Four, along with Mao's 22 strongest Guerrilla Warfare Weapons.
3. Getting into a pissing contest in the first place—this clouds your judgment. If you're going to get into a pissing contest, don't do it because of your heated emotions.

Question 3. This question is not about dumb mistakes. Instead, we're asking you something else. What Deal-Making Weapon is Mao is using now?

Answer: Preparation 2—*Pick your battles carefully—prepare, rehearse, manage your time.*

Question 4. And what dumb mistake is Mao making now?

Answer. Underestimating Trump.

Question 5. What Weapon is Mao thinking about now?

Answer: Assertive 32—*Know your enemy and know yourself—knowledge is power.*

Question 6. What Weapon is Mao thinking about now?

Answer: Preparation 19—*How to make concessions—20 do's and 20 don'ts.*

Question 7. Mao is now using what two Weapons?

Answer:

1. Defensive 24—*Grapevine gossip.*
2. Assertive 95—*Intimidate others if you're a celebrity.*

Question 8. What dumb mistake is Mao making now?

Answer: Wrong assumption—that Trump's subordinates would fail to prepare a written transcript of Mao's remarks in English and give that transcript to Trump.

Question 9. Mao is making another dumb mistake. What is it?

Answer: The same one. Making the wrong assumption. Trump's hotel in Vegas has no casino.

Question 10. What Weapon is Mao using now?

Answer: Dirty Trick 31—*Humiliate and ridicule the other guy.*

Question 11. What dumb mistake is Mao making now?

Answer: Meeting at Trump's office, not at Mao's hotel suite.

Question 12. What Weapon is Trump using now?

Answer: One of Mao's own Guerrilla Weapons. Number 4—*Shock and awe.*

Question 13. Trump is now using what four Dirty Tricks?

Answer:

1. Dirty Trick 31—*Make visitor face the sun—glare and stare.*
2. Dirty Trick 32—*Chairs—yours, high; visitor's, low.*
3. Dirty Trick 33—*Chairs—Yours, stable; visitor's, wobbly.*
4. Dirty Trick 36—*Your meeting room—intimidating décor.*

CHAPTER 2

18 REASONS WHY AMERICANS AREN'T THAT GOOD AT DEAL-MAKING— AND WHAT YOU CAN DO ABOUT IT!

What this chapter is all about: *You'll learn why so many Americans in general are sub-par at deal-making—and why a lot of them stink! You'll also learn how to avoid the dumb mistakes and misguided assumptions many Americans make. Result: We get a lot less than we could when we try to close a deal, especially when we negotiate with foreigners. The rest of your book tells you how to substantially improve your deal-making skills. Oh, and you'll love the part in this chapter about Sam Walton, whom we think is **the ultimate guerrilla***!

Sneak Preview of This Chapter

To a foreigner, all Americans seem to be Big Dogs. We sure act that way. We often seem to be out of touch with the rest of the world—and with each other, as well. For example, people in the desert southwest don't really have much in common with people in the New England states. In Europe, it's different. Nations are much smaller. And so the French feel a sense of kinship with each other when they watch the national weather forecast on TV. That's because they know the weather in Bordeaux (southwest) is usually the same as the weather in Strasbourg (northeast). Don lives near Las Vegas, Nevada, in the middle of the Mojave Desert. Dry all the time. Hot as blazes for five to six months a year. He doesn't care what the weather's like in Boston, Massachusetts, 3,000 miles away from here. He doesn't plan to go there—that's where his ex-wife lives! And Bostonians don't care about weather in Vegas—unless they're getting ready to go there on a trip. America's the third largest nation in the world in terms of land area (after Russia and Canada). We also have the third largest population, after China and India. Our size divides us and isolates us from each other.

For several hundred years, the U.S. was isolated from the rest of the world because of geography. Separated from European and Asian nations by two oceans. Some interaction with Canadians and Mexicans. We were self-sufficient—or at least *thought* we were. We didn't need to trade *too* much with other nations. So we kept to ourselves and developed differently. We're still different. Very different. That was OK for many years. We had all we needed in the U.S.—even though retailers in New Orleans didn't really like dealing with suppliers in New York City. Too different. Today, though, it takes only a few hours to go from San Francisco to London. Ditto New York to Tokyo. Lots of trade between nations. Americans deal with people in other countries on a regular basis now. That's why it's more important than ever for Americans to become better deal-makers with people in different nations. If we Big Dog Americans follow the suggestions we make in your book and adopt a guerrilla attitude, we will win more often.

But right now, most Americans seem to fall short here. What can be done? Here's one way: Try thinking like Mexicans do.

Try Thinking Like Mexicans—They're Natural Guerrillas

A large percentage of Americans come up short at deal-making when you compare them to other nationalities. That's why we often get the short end of the stick when we try to make deals with foreigners. Let's take an American and a Mexican. An American will go into a store, look at the price, and will assume that's the *lowest* price the seller will accept. So the big dog American doesn't haggle. A Mexican will go into the same store, look at the same price, and will assume that's the *highest* price the seller will accept. Haggling is second nature to Mexicans. And second nature to folks like Don, who was born and raised on the Mexican border in bi-cultural Laredo, Texas. Don likes to say, "I think like a Mexican. They're natural guerrillas. And that makes me a better deal-maker. Hell, I'm even one-fourth Mexican myself. *Digo eso con mucho orgullo!*"

Let's take this one step further. One big reason Americans don't win as much as they should when dealing with foreigners and with each other is that we seem to think we're big dogs. We're not natural guerrillas. This is the first of 18 reasons:

18 Reasons Why Americans Are Often Lousy at Getting What They Want

Reason 1. Thinking we're big dogs: Our Santa Claus mentality.

Americans are a mixture of contradictions. Although we're more argumentative, we also like to give away the store to see the other person smile (Assertive Weapon 85, *Act Like Santa Claus—I can afford to give it away*). We pride ourselves at being number one. For example, we're first in exports, imports, retail sales, per capita income, passenger cars, Nobel Prize winners, gross domestic product, number of museums, and many other things. And that's our Achilles Heel—we tend to think like big dogs, not like guerrillas.

You should always remember this: Pride blinds you—when you think you're number one, you also think you can *afford* to make a lot of concessions. Non-Americans think the U.S. is a very rich nation. They perceive us as big dogs, not guerrillas. This makes them want more from Americans, so they try harder to get more. This is a very big disadvantage for us. Don spends a lot of time in the Philippines, where haggling is the norm at most retailers. He knows that when Filipinos see him, they'll start out with a higher price and won't make as many concessions, because they feel he is a rich Americano. So he taught his Filipina wife, Eda, his deal-making tricks, and she almost always does the haggling for him while he hides. She doesn't look like a big dog. He loves to show up at the very end and pay the bill and watch the expressions on the faces of the Filipino sellers when they see the big dog who was lurking behind the scenes.

Reason 2. Big, big need to be liked—an almost paranoid need for lots of affection.

Americans—both guerrillas and big dogs—want to be loved by everybody else, for some strange reason. So we try to do good, all around the world. We try to win other people's affection by giving away too many valuable concessions. Our generosity often doesn't work. Remember the old Beatles' song, *Money Can't Buy Me Love*. So why give away the store just to see the other guy smile?

Reason 3. Americans are too blunt, so we don't have a deal-making culture.

We Americans are too blunt—big dogs more so than guerrillas. We step on other people's toes without knowing it. We arrogantly *shoot first and ask questions later*, like we learned in those cowboy movies we loved when we were kids. So we tend to aggressively go after whatever we want. Our ancestors didn't practice the fine art of haggling very often on the wild frontier. There was a lot more elbow room out there, and so they could move somewhere else when conflicts happen. It's much different in Europe. People live in close quarters. They *had* to learn to negotiate—at an early age. Eventually, making deals through the bargaining process became second nature to them. Not to us, though.

Reason 4. One Ranger, one riot: Individualistic to an extreme.

San Antonio, Texas. 1870s. The wild west. Big riot. Local sheriff couldn't handle it. Sent a telegram to the Texas Rangers in Austin, 80 miles away, asking for help. Next day, the sheriff met the train from Austin. Only one Ranger got off. Sheriff was angry and yelled at the Ranger, "Why did Austin send me just one Ranger?" The Ranger answered, "Only one riot, ain't there?"

Fast-forward to today. Americans seem to have the same attitude—we are too fiercely independent. This was necessary for survival on the wild frontier 150 years ago, but it's not necessary today. This go-it-alone mentality has survived over the years. Whether we're big dogs or guerrillas, Americans seem to think "I can do it myself. I don't need a team." So we're often outnumbered by foreigners who usually send a team to negotiate

Reason 5. Too provincial for our own good.

Most Americans haven't traveled much outside the U.S.—except to Mexico, Canada, and perhaps places in the Caribbean. So we're very provincial, very insular. We don't know the ways of the rest of the world. There are a lot of foreign vultures ready to take advantage of us, whether we're guerrillas or big dogs.

Reason 6. Too naïve.

We're so naively honest, we think the other guy will be honest, too. We even think bribery isn't honest. We can't understand why bribery's an accepted way of life in many foreign nations. Don has seen American truck drivers refuse to give a Mexican customs inspector in Nuevo Laredo, Mexico, a lousy five dollar tip to expedite the processing of papers. One truck driver told Don, "It's against company policy, and I don't want to get in trouble." So the Mexican customs official held up the shipment for a week. That cost the company a *lot* more than five bucks. *Mordidas* are expected in Mexico and other Latin American nations. *Suhol* or *daya* speeds things up considerably in the Philippines. *Dash* is a *must* in Nigeria and other African nations. Likewise, *baksheesh* is expected in MENA (Middle East-North Africa) nations, India, and elsewhere. No money, no honey.

Reason 7. Too informal.

We Americans are *much* too informal. "Just call me John," like John Wayne said in many of his western movies. We like to go on a first-name basis. We wonder why business cards of most foreigners only give initials for their first names, not their full given names. We are puzzled when we see the same thing in foreign phone books. We think, "Why don't they put their first name (given name) on their business cards, in their phone books. That would make people easier to find." We don't realize that many non-Americans don't want just *anybody* to know their given name. They'll reveal it to the right person at the right time. It's a privilege only they can bestow. It's a minor privilege, but it's still a privilege. By the way, what's on *your* business card?

Our informality leads to an emphasis on equality in the U.S. We don't understand that foreigners value formality and prestige. And we don't like long introductions. They make us impatient. "Just call me John," indeed!

Reason 8. Too impatient.

Don's been married to two Filipinas. (Not at the same time, of course.) Both of them have the same complaint about him: He's too impatient. He's like most Americans. We get to the point too quickly. Once again, the wild west influenced us. There was a long distance between people in those days. This led to fewer interactions and a much shorter deal-making process.

Here's a big lesson Don learned, told in his own words:

Time Is *Not* Money

I made a big mistake when I was first started out as a *hired gun* negotiator back in the middle 1970s. I kept looking at my watch while talking to a wealthy Chinese business executive in Singapore. Finally, he asked me, "Dr. Hendon, why do you look at your watch so much?" I told him, "Well, time is money." He said, gently, "No, Dr. Hendon. Time is eternity."

That taught me a big lesson—I never wanted to look at my watch again because I didn't want to give out a subtle signal of impatience. In fact, I took it off my wrist and put it in my pocket, in front of the other person, so he would know "My time is yours." (This is Don's Assertive Weapon 113.)

I also learned that many Asians think Americans are apprehensive when they look at their watches. So they take even longer in their deal-making sessions with Americans, in order to reassure us and relieve us of our apprehensions. Guerrillas seem to be more impatient than big dogs.

Reason 9. The one-thing-at-a-time attitude—Even more impatience.

Most Americans like to deal with tasks by separating issues and settling them one at a time. We say, "We've agreed on this, now let's go on to the next item." Don has noticed over the years that non-Americans often commit themselves only at the *very end* of the deal-making process. This makes us Americans even *more* impatient, because we think no progress is being made. And it makes the overall process a series of small conflicts instead of a series of positive steps toward a peaceful and mutually-agreeable solution. However, remember this: When there's a lot of small conflicts, guerrillas have the advantage over the big dogs.

Reason 10. Shame—Very little or no sense of shame.

Both of Don's Filipina wives also complain that he doesn't seem to care very much if he loses face or not. And most Americans share this trait—especially when we deal with foreigners. This might be OK for people who don't care about being laughed at behind their backs. But it's tragic when we Americans don't realize how important saving face is to foreigners—this makes us offend foreigners without realizing it. Big dogs are more conscious about saving face than guerrillas. Here's a warning to you guerrillas reading this—big dogs have an advantage over you in this area.

If you deal with foreigners often, you need to know more about Don's Dirty Trick 81, *Thick face, black heart*, which discusses this in more detail. It's not one of the 100 most powerful of Don's 365 tactical Weapons, though. You can learn more about it in his *365 Powerful Ways* book or by going to **www. GuerrillaDon.com**. His website gives more details about this Weapon than his book does.

Reason 11. Too predictable.

Foreigners know a lot about the U.S. and Americans from our movies and TV programs. They're very popular overseas. So non-Americans know what to expect from Americans because of the influence the U.S. has on popular culture throughout the world. And their expectations are often correct. But foreign movies and foreign TV programs aren't very popular in the U.S. This means Americans are at a big disadvantage when we deal-make, because we don't know what to expect from non-Americans. Remember, many foreigners seem to treat all American negotiators like big dogs. If you're a natural guerrilla, you can take advantage of this by doing things the guerrilla way—foreigners won't know how to handle this, and this gives you more power.

Reason 12. Too argumentative.

Americans are more argumentative than most nationalities. We hate to lose. We not only *want* to win—we *love* to win, to *overwhelm* other people. Americans developed this combative attitude in athletics in primary and secondary school. And this combative attitude was reinforced at business schools where we got our BBAs and MBAs. So Americans keep going and going and going. Non-Americans expect this. They can predict it. They make allowances for it in advance. So be a true guerrilla—put the foreigner off-balance by being more agreeable than argumentative from time to time.

Reason 13. Silence—a terrible attitude toward it.

We Americans are uncomfortable with silence, and so we avoid using Don's Defensive Weapon 10, *Complete, total silence*. Big dogs and guerrillas alike. We try to fill the silent gaps with talk—our talk. This is Defensive Weapon 58. And so, many non-Americans, especially Asians, keep silent on purpose. They know that's a good way of getting Americans to open their mouths. Talking is actually a *huge* concession. If you talk a lot, you're giving the other person lots of information without getting anything in return. That's a dumb mistake—never make a concession without getting something in return. (See Preparation Weapon 19 in Chapter 10. Also see Chapter 17, which is all about making concessions the right way.) Don't give away information without getting something in return from the other person. We've heard an expression since we were little boys: Those inscrutable Orientals. They're *not* inscrutable. They're *smart!*

Reason 14. The take-it-back attitude.

Americans have a tendency to take back something that has already been agreed to. Big dogs do this more than guerrillas. This attitude comes from the deep-seated belief that anything goes until the final contract is signed. Non-Americans resent this, and it makes them resist our demands. Here's what they think: A deal is a deal on each clause. When you read Chapter 17, you'll realize this is one reason so many non-Americans really dislike concession pattern seven. Skip ahead to this chapter if you want and see what this is all about.

Reason 15. Assuming American English is the only kind of English that's spoken.

Before you look at this table, cover up the right column with a sheet of paper or your hand if you're an American. If you're from a British Commonwealth country, cover up the left column. See if you can figure out what these words mean. For example, a lorry (British) is a truck (American). Mincemeat (British) is hamburger (American). And so forth. This will be very frustrating for Americans—but a lot of fun, too. Count how many you got right and how many you got wrong. We'll bet most Americans get them wrong.

British English	American English
Lorry	Truck
Mincemeat	Hamburger
Chicken flesh	Goose pimples
Cot	Baby crib
Roadside dressing	Soft shoulder
Ground floor	First floor
First floor	Second floor
Boot	Trunk
Bonnet	Hood
Tin opener	Can opener
Rising damp	Humidity
Drawing pin	Thumbtack
Scone	Biscuit
Biscuit	Cookie

We're sure you had fun with this exercise. The audiences at Don's seminars love it! But there's a serious side, too. Some words are dangerous when you are making a deal—like *overdraft* and *table it*:

Overdraft = Non-sufficient funds (American)
Overdraft = Line of credit (British)
Table it = Postpone it (American)
Table it = Discuss it now (British)

The British know that we Americans use a slightly different kind of English than they do. But we Americans assume our brand of English is universal. This puts Americans at a big disadvantage when we try to make a deal in the U.K. and British Commonwealth nations. Become a true guerrilla—learn the idioms in each country, and don't make the wrong assumptions.

Reason 16. The English language is a bad language to use when you're dealing with people whose native language isn't English.

Three reasons:

- Ambiguity: It's not ambiguous enough. *Yes* always means *yes*, and *no* always means *no*. Japanese use *hai* to mean many things: Yes, I understand you. Yes, I don't understand you. Yes, I'll do it. Yes, I won't do it. And so forth. Americans don't realize this is happening.
- Local translators: Americans are at the mercy of translators when they go overseas. We strongly urge you to hire your *own* translators. Don't be a *cheap* guerrilla. Don't use the translators provided by the company you're negotiating with. Why ask for trouble?
- Universal understanding vs. selective understanding: Most business executives outside the U.S. understand English. It's the international language of business. But many of them pretend they don't understand English. Most Americans speak only English. So, it's easier for non-Americans to eavesdrop on Americans than for Americans to eavesdrop on non-Americans. And non-Americans like to have things translated into their language, even though they don't need it. This gives them more time to think, to evaluate the Americans, and to come up with a response. Don does this a lot in Latin American nations. When he's shopping, he pretends he doesn't understand

Spanish and eavesdrops on what the store employees are saying to this *pendejo*, this *gringo estupido*. Once he knows their bottom line, he zaps them with his fluent Spanish and gets a great deal. (See Don's Assertive Weapon 17.)

Reason 17. Much too aggressive in almost every situation

Here are five characteristics of an aggressive person. Ask yourself if these are the same characteristics of Americans in general? Of big dogs? Of guerrillas?

- Brave: They function well in difficult and dangerous situations. They're not distracted by fear.
- Command: They're comfortable with power, authority, and responsibility. So they try to take charge as soon as possible.
- Disciplined: They impose rules and expect others to follow them.
- Expedient, goal-directed, and practical: They do whatever's necessary to get the job done.
- Sense of order: They operate best within an environment where there are clear lines of authority and everyone knows his place.

We think these are characteristics of Americans in general and that they have been for a long time. For example, here are three excerpts from the *London Morning Chronicle* in 1852, commenting on what they thought was an impending invasion of Cuba by the U.S.:

- Reckless adventurers infest the U.S.
- Most Americans, intoxicated with prosperity and lending a greedy ear to the flattery of demagogues, believe that the empire of the New World belongs to them.
- An aggressive spirit is a major part of the American character.

Do you agree with us? And were Americans more aggressive and guerrilla-like in the 1800s than today?

Reason 18. Much too arrogant—We're right, the rest of the world is wrong!

Not only are we more aggressive, we also seem to be arrogant. Especially big dogs. We have one big blind spot that tends to make us that way. Here's a survey that shows how much the U.S. is out-of-step with a lot of the rest of the world—big-time!

It was taken between November 12 and December 13, 2001—two months after the September 11 terrorist attacks on the World Trade Center. And one month after the U.S. invaded Afghanistan (on October 7, 2001). The survey concerned the American invasion of Afghanistan. Here are four of the questions that were asked:

Question	Americans— percent saying yes	Non-Americans— percent saying yes
If Iraq has supported terrorism, should the U.S. attack that country?	50	29
Were U.S. policies a major cause of the September 11 attacks?	0	26
Does the U.S. do a lot of good around the world?	52	21
Did the U.S. ignore the interests of its partner nations in its war on terrorism?	28	62

Here's more evidence that we Americans march to a different drummer when it comes to getting others to do what we want them to do. As we said earlier, Don has gathered data from thousands of business executives in more than 60 nations on six continents in his seminars on deal-making. He asked his participants which tactical Weapons they liked to use in 11 different deal-making situations—five business, five personal, and dealing with a hostile attorney. This last one could be either personal or business. Here are results from the U.S. and from ten other nations—contrasting Americans' favorite Weapons with favorite Weapons used by 11 other nationalities:

Deal-making situation	Americans	Executives in Other Nations
Seller: Get buyer to pay more	Size matters—the big pot (Assertive 48)	*Chile*: Threaten doomsday (Assertive 112)
Buyer: Get seller to lower the price	Say "Take it or leave it" and be prepared to walk away—Elvis has left the building (Assertive 68)	*Britain* and *Australia*: Remind the other person of his competition—real or imaginary (Defensive 4)
Ask your boss for a raise	Hey, let's look at the record (Assertive 104)	*Brazil*: Find allies and use them (Defensive 76)
Ask your boss for a promotion	Hey, let's look at the record (Assertive 104)	*New Zealand*: Go *way* beyond what you *have* to do (Cooperative 21)
Change your vacation date	Anticipate his objections and defuse them in advance (Defensive 13)	*Thailand*: Make promises instead of conceding (Cooperative 13)
Deal with a hostile attorney	Control the agenda (Assertive 53)	*Indonesia*: The power of powerlessness and creeping paralysis (Defensive 1)
Buy a house	Size matters—the big pot (Assertive 48)	*Philippines*: Remind him of his competition—real or imaginary (Defensive 4)
Sell your car	Size matters—the big pot (Assertive 48)	*Malaysia*: Say "Take it or leave it" and be prepared to walk away—Elvis has left the building (Assertive 68)
Get out of a traffic ticket	Admit your mistakes and apologize before he tries to blame you (Defensive 85)	*Kenya*: Bribe him (Dirty Trick 20)

Get your children to pick up their clothes	Momentum: Always keep pressure on them (Assertive 66)	*Hong Kong*: Intimidate him by making them feel guilty (Assertive 80)
Sexual favors from a friend		

You'll notice Don left the last situation blank. Why? Because this is the only situation where almost everybody in those 36 nations—including Americans—agreed. But it's also the only situation where men were very different from women. Men really liked to use *Smooth talk, flattery, and charm* (Assertive 60), while women loved to use *Make men aware of their competition—real or imaginary* (Defensive 4). That's because, almost everywhere, men are the pursuers and women are the pursued.

If you would like to have specific details of favorite tactical Weapons used in these 11 situations by people in different nations, by men versus women, by big dogs versus guerrillas, etc., please go to **www.GuerrillaDon.com** for details.

How Anybody Can Become a Big Winner—Think Small! Sam Walton Did!

If you're an American, these 18 reasons should make you re-evaluate yourself. Begin with the first reason: Thinking we're big dogs—the Santa Claus mentality. If you've got a big ego, get rid of it. Thinking—and acting—like you're number one makes people want more from you, and this puts you at a big disadvantage when you're trying to make a deal. Think small instead. That means thinking the way guerrillas think. One of Don's 50 most powerful and *under*-used Weapons you'll read about in Chapter Five is Preparation 16, *Think small*. Guerrillas use it in war, and that's one of the main reasons they're so successful. Business people who think like guerrillas use it, too, with equal success. Here's why:

As Don says in his seminars:

"Smaller businesses are natural guerrillas—they can do almost anything they want because they've got *very little* to lose. Large businesses, on the other hand, often feel they have very few choices because they've got *too much* to lose. And so they're a lot more cautious. It's hard to get executives in large businesses to think like guerrillas, to think small. And so smaller guerrillas can do *anything*. They can run circles around the big dogs. They take advantage of the big dog's paralysis of caution."

To think small and be successful at the same time, you need a lot of imagination and creativity. Like Sam Walton, the founder of Wal-Mart. He was a natural guerrilla. He wasn't afraid to fail. But then again, he had a great idea and was small enough to implement it without getting stepped on by the giants of retailing. Like Mao, he started in the countryside, owned it, and eventually moved to the big cities. And he beat the big dogs of the time—Kmart (still around but not nearly as dominant as it was), Woolco (long gone), E. J. Korvette (ditto), and other big discount store chains. Here's the story of the most successful guerrilla businessman of all time, as told by Don in his negotiating and deal-making seminars. It's everybody's favorite handout.

Thinking Small Is Really Thinking Big— the Sam Walton Success Story

Sam Walton is the *ultimate guerrilla*. We dedicate Chapter 18 to him. He owned a series of small five-and-ten-cent-variety stores in northwestern Arkansas in the 1940s and 1950s. Eventually, he and his brother Ben ran 16 stores in that part of the U.S.—Arkansas, Missouri, and Kansas. He was losing customers to discount chain stores such as Woolco and Kmart, even though they were located in larger cities over 100 miles away. People from Bentonville, where he was headquartered, drove over dangerous winding mountain roads to go to Little Rock, Fort Smith, Springfield, Joplin, Tulsa, and Kansas City where the discount stores were. He couldn't match the chains' low prices—his stores were too small to buy in bulk. So he decided to outmaneuver them by coming up with a bold and daring idea that cost him a lot of his assets:

He figured that three stores the size of his original Ben Franklin store in Bentonville would match the buying power of a smaller Woolco or Kmart. So he set up a small warehouse in the center of several small towns in Arkansas. He bought in sufficient bulk that he could match the prices of Woolco's and Kmart's in those larger cities. He opened his first Wal-Mart in Bentonville in 1962. The big chains ignored him. They didn't want to invade smaller cities anyway. They, like Chiang Kai-Shek in China, were too cautious to go after their enemies in the countryside. And they eventually lost the war.

Sam took advantage of the big chains' indifference and kept expanding. He set up more and more warehouses, and added more and more retail stores. He stuck to small towns. Eventually, like Mao Tse Tung and Le Duan, the guerrilla architect of North Viet Nam's victory over the U.S. and South Viet Nam, he decided to attack the large cities in force. He started in Philadelphia, and Wal-Mart there was a big winner. By then, he was too big to be stopped by the big discount chains. He began opening Wal-Marts in the outer suburbs of large cities, where land was cheaper. His stores were larger than the Woolco's and Kmart's. Economies of scale. Americans were moving away from the cities into the suburbs and outer suburbs, where Sam opened his Wal-Mart's. The older Woolco's and Kmart's weren't as large, clean, and attractive as the newer Wal-Marts, and they had higher rental and insurance rates. With their higher operating costs, they couldn't match Wal-Mart's efficiencies and had to charge higher prices.

Eventually, Wal-Mart became the number one retailer in the world. Woolco went out of business. Kmart merged with Sears. Other big discounters went out of business, too. Anybody remember E. J. Korvette, a giant discount chain in the northeastern U.S.? Long gone. How about GEM? Treasure Island? Richway? Ditto. The moral of the story: *Thinking small is actually thinking big.* Think like winners—think small! Even if you're with a big company! You'll win more.

By the way, Jay reprinted Don's story about Sam Walton in his 2011 book, *Guerrilla Marketing Remix* on pages 179-180.

What's Coming Up in Chapter Three

Americans are too blunt, individualistic, provincial, honest, informal, impatient, predictable, argumentative, and naïve. We think like Santa Claus, want others to like us, have almost no sense of shame, hate silence, and have ideas on signing contracts that most other nationalities don't have. On top of that, English is so universal, it's a bad language to negotiate in. How can you overcome all this? You have to get inside the minds of the big dogs. That's how to win. And that's what Chapter Three is all about.

CHAPTER 3

KNOW YOUR ENEMY—HOW TO GET INSIDE THE BIG DOG'S MIND

What this chapter is all about: *Here, you learn what's going on inside the mind of the big dog, the powerful opponent guerrillas face in the deal-making process. After you read this chapter, you'll know how to take advantage of the big dog's Big I, Little You attitude. You'll learn many subtle tricks to win him over to your side.*

Does this title grab your attention? That's why we used it. To *really* get inside the big dog's mind, let's travel back in time 8,000 years. Some of you may have heard of Sun Tzu. He's the ancient Chinese warrior, whose book, *The Art of War*, is still in print. His most famous saying is "Know your enemy and know yourself, and you'll win every battle." The title of Don's Assertive Weapon 32 is a paraphrase of this: *Know your enemy and know yourself— knowledge is power*, and we discuss it in Chapter Five. Sun Tzu's advice is still good today. Know as much as you can about the big dog you're dealing with. And by getting rid of your blind spots, you'll know yourself.

However, please remember this: Although the big dog is on the other side of the negotiating table from you, he is *not* your enemy. As Jay said in *Guerrilla Marketing Excellence*, the underlying concept of a guerrilla relationship is the success of your customer, the big dog. You don't want to destroy him, to humiliate him. You need to contribute to his success, and if you do, you'll be successful, too. How do you contribute to his success? Here are seven suggestions. In descending order of strength:

What Guerrillas Should Do	Results in the Big Dog You'll Notice Right Away
Give him good ideas he can use to make more profits	He appreciates this more than anything else
Give him important information about his customers—information that will help him sell more to them	This delights him
Give him price breaks	This makes him very, very happy
Pay a lot of attention to him	This flatters him
Make him feel special, unique, one-of-a-kind after each sales call you make	This is good for his ego
Invite him to seminars which you know will give him good new ideas	This pleases him
Don't rely on your jokes too much	If they're good, he'll be amused. But your jokes don't contribute to his success

Most stuff in books written about how big dogs become successful have nothing but generalities and platitudes in them. Such as

- They aren't reckless. They take calculated risks instead.
- They think positively. "Think and grow rich," as Napoleon Hill said so long ago.
- They don't blame others when things go wrong.
- They're persistent. They come back from setbacks and try, try again.
- They have vision, whatever that means.

You've got to know as much as possible about the big dog you're dealing with, but how much do you think these generalities will help you win? Not much. Instead, let's go inside the mind of big dogs and see how you can get them to consider and adopt your ideas.

First Impressions

Let's assume you and the big dog have an appointment. (If you don't have an appointment, Don's Assertive Weapon 34 gives you good advice on how to get past over-protective gatekeepers. Title: *Use gatekeepers—yours and his*.) Ideally, your meeting should be in your office, but it probably won't be— you're the guerrilla, and the big dog thinks you need him more than he needs you. And so he makes a power play by making you come to him. Don't be surprised if the big dog uses guerrilla-like Weapons on you. Look for such things as:

- Where your chair is placed. Directly opposite the big dog is confrontational. Diagonally is friendlier.
- If his chair is higher than yours, watch out!
- If your chair is wobbly, watch out!
- Watch out if the window is behind him and the sun is glaring into your eyes.
- If large formal photos or oil-paintings of the big dog and company officials, watch out!
- If the room temperature is too hot or too cold, watch out.
- If there are many interruptions, watch out! The big dog may have a silent buzzer under his desk to get his secretary to interrupt your meeting.
- His overall office layout. If he occupies most of the space and his visitors are forced into a small space, he's trying to dominate you. More information about this is in *Use position power—the language spoken by office furniture* in Chapter 16. This is Don's Defensive Weapon 19.

Notice we said these are guerrilla-*like* Weapons. They're too obvious for *real* guerrillas to use. They're for guerrilla *wanna-be's*. Many big dogs secretly admire guerrillas and subconsciously wish they were adventurous enough to become more like guerrillas One giveaway is what hobbies they have. For example, if they ride motorcycles on weekends, they're probably guerrilla wanna-be's. And wanting to be more like you, the guerrilla, is one of their biggest weaknesses. Eventually, you'll learn how to exploit that! But first, you've got to get the big dog to listen seriously to you.

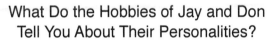

What Do the Hobbies of Jay and Don Tell You About Their Personalities?

Jay's hobbies: Skiing. Car and RV exploring throughout North America. Poker. Trivia. Chicago White Sox.

Don's hobbies: Collecting Uncle $crooge McDuck memorabilia, including McDuck license plates. Motorcycle-riding and dune buggying. Golf. Swimming. Juggling. Poker and chess. Performer at amateur nights at various comedy clubs in the U.S.

How to Get the Big Dog Not Only to Listen Seriously to You but Also Accept Your Proposal

First of all, you've got to knock him off his power pedestal somehow. When the big dog is feeling the power of his position, he probably won't listen to you—at least, not seriously.

Powerful people have confidence in what they are thinking. So when you're trying to get the big dog to accept your arguments, you've got to shake his confidence without being obvious about it. Here are six ways to do this. Which one do you think is the best? Which is the worst?

- Attack his strongly-held beliefs. Use sound logic.
- Make a strong argument.
- Massage his ego.
- Put the big dog in a situation where he doesn't feel as powerful. Temporarily. But if you try to make this less-powerful feeling last too long, he will resent it and may kick you out of the office.
- Remind him of his power *after* you make your argument.
- Remind him of his power *before* you make your argument.

Look for our answers at the end of this chapter. In the meantime, here's what you should know about how to get the big dog to listen to your new idea:

Power is really an aphrodisiac. It makes big dogs more likely to believe their own thoughts and then act on them. And so if you temporarily *make a powerful person feel less powerful, less confident,* you have a much better chance of getting him to pay attention to your arguments. Here's how Don does it:

- Say something that temporarily shakes his confidence. Like bringing up something he doesn't know—something that makes him feel less certain. That reduces his confidence.
- But don't shake his confidence tree too much, or he might throw you out of his office. A good way to do this is to pick the correct location. Try to persuade him when he's *not* in his office. It's easier to shake his confidence if he's not in his comfortable office with so many symbols of power all around him.
- Remember this: The strength of your argument is a lot less important in convincing him than shaking his confidence in his infallibility. And when he starts to realize he's not infallible, he'll pay more attention to what you are saying. A *lot* more.

But it's not enough just to get the big dog to pay attention to you. The second hurdle is to get him to feel infallible again right after you make your argument. When the big dog again feels powerful, he has more confidence in *his most recent thoughts—the stuff you told him, in other words.* So flatter his ego by reminding him he's still in charge.

Here's the step-by-step way to do this: When you do these three things in order, you'll probably get the big dog to change his mind:

- Shake his confidence—temporarily.
- Make a pretty good argument.
- Bring back his confidence by reminding him he's still in charge. He'll again feel powerful enough to accept your argument without any doubt.

The Ultimate Guerrilla

Reminding him he's still in charge is the most important thing of all. Here's how to do it without being too obvious about it—become the *ultimate guerrilla*. Emulate Sam Walton, as we said in Chapter Two.

How do you become the ultimate guerrilla? And what *is* the *ultimate guerrilla*, anyway? There are a lot of potential Sam Walton's out there. Let's find out by looking at these three phrases:

- Right and wrong are just words. What matters is what you do.

- If you do too much, people get dependent on you. And if you do nothing, they lose hope. You have to use a light touch.
- When you do things right, people won't be sure you've done anything at all.

If they sound somewhat familiar to you, you, like Don are probably a fan of *Futurama*, a series on Comedy Channel and other networks. It's a very funny cartoon set in the year 3000. Its creator is the same guy who created *The Simpsons*. The main character is Bender, a robot who curses, fights, argues, steals, smokes cigars, drinks, and gambles. He works at Planet Express, which is similar to FedEx, UPS, and DHL. The three phrases were taken from its *Godfellas* episode, which was first shown on Fox TV in 2002.

> Bender gets shot into deep outer space by mistake. A small colony of humanoids start growing on his body. They begin to worship him as God. He tries to help the people by doing what the real God would do—but with disastrous consequences. Everybody suffers and dies. Later on, as he continues traveling through deep space, he meets the real God. Here's some dialog:
>
> Bender: I'll bet a lot of people pray to you, huh?
>
> God: Yes, but there are so many, asking so much. After a while, you just sort of tune it out.
>
> Bender: You know, I was God once. It was awful. I tried helping them. I tried *not* helping them. But in the end, I couldn't do them any good. Do you think what I did was wrong?
>
> God: Right and wrong are just words. What matters is what you do. Being God isn't easy. If you do too much, people get dependent on you. If you do nothing, they lose hope. You have to use a light touch, like a safecracker, or a pickpocket. When you do things right, people won't be sure you've done anything at all.

Don has been following this philosophy, subconsciously, a long time before he ever saw the *Godfellas* episode. You should, too. Become the *ultimate guerrilla* by always remembering to use a light touch. *When you do things right, others won't be sure you've done anything at all* (Don's Preparation Weapon 31).

Easy to say, hard to do, especially if you have a big ego. Our advice: *Lose your ego* (Preparation 10).

Who do *we* think is the ultimate guerrilla? You already know! Sam Walton, the founder of Wal-Mart. We told you why we respect him so much in Chapter Two.

What You Learned Here and What's Coming Up Next

Did you get inside the big dog's mind in this chapter? We hope so. You learned what guerrillas should do to make the big dog realize you're contributing to his success, what your first impressions tell you about him, how to get him listen seriously to you and accept your proposal, and how to become the *ultimate guerrilla*. So what's coming up next? The heart and soul of your book: A directory of Don's 365 mainstream tactical Weapons and 22 of Mao's most powerful guerrilla Weapons in Chapter Four. Then, the 100 most powerful of Don's 365 Weapons: The 50 most *under*-used ones in Chapters 5-9, and the 50 most *over*-used ones in Chapters 10-15. Before going there, though, read the answer to how to get the big dog to listen seriously to you:

How to Get the Big Dog to Listen Seriously to You—Answer

From best to worst:

- Best: Put the big dog in a situation where he doesn't feel as powerful. Temporarily. But if you try to make this less-powerful feeling last too long, he will resent it and may kick you out of the office.
- Second best: Remind him of his power *after* you make your argument.
- Neutral: Make a strong argument.
- Neutral: Massage the big dog's ego.
- Next-to-worst: Remind him of his power *before* you make your argument.
- Worst: Attack his strongly-held beliefs. Use sound logic.

PART TWO

DONALD WAYNE HENDON'S MOST POWERFUL INFLUENCE WEAPONS AND MAO TSE-TUNG'S MOST POWERFUL GUERRILLA WARFARE WEAPONS

CHAPTER 4

DON AND MAO—THEIR MOST POWERFUL WEAPONS

Donald Wayne Hendon's
365 Powerful Deal-Making Weapons

Copyright (c) 2001-2012 by Dr. Donald Wayne Hendon

 00 Weapons are in bold-face. They are the most powerful of the 365 Weapons and are the ones we talk about in Chapters 5-15. 50 are **under-used**, and 50 are *over-used*—by both guerrillas and big dogs.

31 Preparation Weapons

How to begin preparing (7 Weapons, 1-7)

1. Think ahead—circumstances are always changing
2. Pick your battles carefully—prepare, rehearse, manage your time
3. Avoid paralysis of perfectionism—set priorities. Use the 80-20 rule
4. **Overcome the paralysis of not thinking fast enough by learning from children (Under-used)**
5. **The right attitude—I've got to earn the right to learn TOS's needs (Under-used)** *Note*: Remember, TOS stands for the other side or the other person

6.   Empathy—put yourself in TOS's place
7.   Become hard to convince

What to do about your ego (4 Weapons, 8-11)
8.   **Don't give away the store just to see TOS smile (Under-used)**
9.   Blind spots—know yours and TOS's
10. Deal with your ego
11. **Mistakes—admit them, learn from them (Under-used)**

What to do about your tensions and negative emotions (2 Weapons, 12-13)
12. Calm down and lighten up
13. **The Escalation Commitment—throwing good money after bad is just plain stupid (Under-used)**

Be daring (3 Weapons, 14-16)
14. Dare to fail
15. Prepare, trust your instincts, then do it
16. **Think small (Under-used)**

Commitment and integrity (2 Weapons, 17-18)
17. Commit yourself totally
18. Integrity—never lose it

Making concessions (1 Weapon, 19)
19. *How to make concessions: 20 Do's and 20 Don'ts (Over-used)*

What's the best order? (4 Weapons, 20-23)
20. Order: Easiest first, hardest last
21. Order: Hardest first, easiest last
22. Gain momentum by making first offer yourself
23. *Show me yours, then I'll show you mine (Over-used)*

The finishing touches (6 Weapons, 24-29)
24. Don't be too satisfied when it's over—stay a little hungry
25. Be in good physical condition

26. **Negotiate on an empty stomach (Under-used)**

27. **Make deals in the morning, not in the afternoon (Under-used)**

28. TOS's objections—be curious, not angry or sad

29. Passion and enthusiasm are contagious

The master strategist (2 Weapons, 30-31)

30. Learn and master chess

31. When you do things right, people won't be sure you did anything at all

121 Assertive Weapons

Distraction (22 Weapons in 4 parts, 1-22)

Part 1. The basic weapon (1 Weapon)

1. Make sudden, unexpected moves (Under-used)

Part 2. General surprises (9 Weapons, 2-10)

2. Attack TOS's ego—abuse by sarcasm

3. Surprise TOS with your expert

4. Surprise TOS with new information

5. Surprise TOS with new issues and broader problems

6. Bipolar negotiation—very abrupt mood swings

7. New leader, no leader

8. Strange changes in your team's makeup

9. Time surprises—change deadlines

10. Location surprises—frequent changes (meeting rooms, addresses, even cities)

Part 3. Pretending (6 Weapons, 11-16)

11. ***Playing dumb is smart. Say "Who, me? Sorry, I didn't know" (Over-used)***

12. Eavesdrop by faking ignorance of language

13. Fake ignorance of local customs

14. I believe you, you liar

15. ***Act astonished! (Over-used)***

16. Show pain when you concede

Part 4. 6 other distractions (6 Weapons, 17-22)

17. **Turn your liabilities into assets—then** *zap!* **TOS at the end (Under-used)**
18. **Put on a good show by acting wild and crazy (Under-used)**
19. *Don't give TOS your best offer too soon (Over-used)*
20. **For sellers: Make buyers pursue you for a change (Under-used)**
21. When TOS is angry, distract him
22. Flirting—attract, reject, then attract again

Moderately Assertive (28 Weapons in 5 parts, 23-50)
Part 1. Time (6 weapons, 23-28)

23. When to speak, when to pause
24. *Avoid buyer's remorse—don't accept TOS's first offer too quickly (Over-used)*
25. **A Chinese favorite—the rule of three (Under-used)**
26. Extend negotiations over long periods of time
27. **Learn from car dealers—make TOS invest a lot of his time (Under-used)**
28. *Use deadlines wisely (Over-used)*

Part 2. Knowledge (5 Weapons, 29-33)

29. Be suspicious at first—look for and recognize TOS's 12 smokescreens, 11 shields, and 14 scams
30. Take advantage of these 37 smokescreens, shills, shields, scams/cons—creatively
31. *Detect TOS's blind spots and take advantage of them (Over-used)*
32. **Know your enemy and know yourself—knowledge is power (Under-used)**
33. Be logical—and make sure TOS knows you are

Part 3. Involving other people (4 Weapons, 34-37)

34. Use gatekeepers—yours and his
35. *Stay powerful—divide and conquer (Over-used)*
36. **Turn TOS's top assistants into heroes (Under-used)**

37. Use a professional or agent to assist you in negotiating—if you're inexperienced

Part 4. Bragging and anti-bragging (6 Weapons, 38-43)
38. *Act arrogant—overwhelm TOS by pulling rank (Over-used)*
39. *Act egotistical—I'm the greatest! (Over-used)*
40. The bandwagon effect—lead a parade
41. **Imply your power—don't intentionally *display* it (Under-used)**
42. Dress very well
43. Dress sloppy on purpose

Part 5. 6 very transparent Weapons, plus a surprise (7 Weapons, 44-50)
44. **Good guy, bad guy (Over-used)**
45. **Scare, then rescue TOS (Under-used)**
46. Make TOS depend on you—easier to manipulate him
47. *Use a decoy to divert attention away from what you really want (Over-used)*
48. *Size matters—the big pot (Over-used)*
49. Auctions—the little pot
50. *Bluffing—not-too-obvious lying (Over-used)*

Confrontation, control, and overwhelm (9 Weapons in 3 parts, 51-59)
Part 1. Confrontation (2 Weapons, 51-52)
51. Confront TOS—call his bluff
52. Confront TOS again—ask, "Why are you using Dirty Tricks, and when will you stop?"

Part 2. Control (3 Weapons, 53-55)
53. Control the agenda
54. Control the agreement process itself
55. Limit what your team can tell TOS

Part 3. Overwhelm (4 Weapons, 56-59)
56. *Wish lists vs. reality lists (Over-used)*
57. Negotiate where you have the most power—your place
58. *Tuangou / swarming ambush / flash mobs (Under-used)*

59. Size of your negotiating team—be bigger than their team

White lies, borderline aggression, and the power of *no* (13 Weapons in 3 parts, 60-72)
Part 1. White lies (3 Weapons, 60-62)
60. *Use smooth talk, charm, and flattery (Over-used)*
61. *Convince TOS you have lots of general information, even if you don't (Over-used)*
62. Exaggerate slightly, but not too much

Part 2. Borderline aggression (8 Weapons, 63-70)
63. Get paid first, then perform
64. **Take it first, then talk about it (Under-used)**
65. Watch out for scams—never pay in advance
66. *Momentum: Always keep pressure on TOS (Over-used)*
67. Powerful ultimatum
68. *Say "Take it or leave it" and be prepared to walk away—Elvis has left the building (Over-used)*
69. Make TOS realize you're *very* committed to your goals
70. Be brave, not scared

Part 3. Power of *no* (2 Weapons, 71-72)
71. Be stubborn—say *no*
72. *Never accept a* **no** *from TOS (Over-used)*

Just plain mean and nasty Weapons (29 Weapons in 4 parts, 73-101)
Part 1. Threats (5 Weapons, 73-77)
73. *Tell TOS you're getting ready to withdraw from the deal (Over-used)*
74. Tell TOS you're going over his head
75. Tell TOS you're *going public*—soon, everybody will know
76. Tell TOS you're going to tell government officials—police, regulatory agencies, etc.
77. Threaten TOS with actual physical violence

Part 2. Obvious intimidation (18 Weapons, 78-89)

78. ***Intimidate TOS by tradition, custom, and conformity (Over-used)***
79. Intimidate TOS by superstitions, slogans, and proverbs
80. ***Intimidate TOS by making him feel guilty (Over-used)***
81. Intimidate TOS by slandering him
82. Intimidate TOS by name-calling, stereotyping
83. Intimidate TOS by your height, especially if you are unusually tall
84. Intimidate TOS by your money
85. Act like Santa Claus—I can afford to give it away
86. Intimidate TOS by lawful, legitimate power
87. Intimidate TOS by your charisma
88. ***Intimidate TOS by rewarding or punishing him (Over-used)***
89. Intimidate TOS by using big words

Part 3. Envy (6 Weapons, 90-95)

90. Intimidate TOS by your titles and status in the company
91. Intimidate TOS by your credentials
92. Intimidate TOS by your prestigious occupation
93. **Intimidate TOS by being untouchable (Under-used)**
94. Intimidate TOS by your expertise or by bringing an expert with you
95. Intimidate TOS if you're a celebrity

Part 4. Subtle intimidation (6 Weapons, 96-101)

96. Communication—change from direct to indirect
97. ***Put TOS on the defensive—accuse him, make negative statements, and... (Over-used)***
98. Make stupid *major* mistakes on purpose
99. Make it easy for TOS to make stupid mistakes
100. **Ignore TOS—have a *deaf ear* (Under-used)**
101. *Pretend* to lose your temper

Endurance (3 Weapons, 102-104)

102. The squeaky wheel—flexible persistence
103. ***Nibble away—wear out TOS, outlast him (Over-used)***

104. *Hey, let's look at the record (Over-used)*

Foot-in-the-door (3 Weapons, 105-107)
105. Foot in the door—barely
106. Foot in the door—then, wiggle your toes
107. Foot in the door—then, kick door down

Games played by both grown-ups and children (5 Weapons, 108-112)
108. Think and become more like a child
109. Use *rock, paper, scissors* to break deadlocks
110. Cry on purpose—sympathy-seeking to the extreme
111. Dares and the game of *Chicken*
112. Threaten doomsday

9 other Assertive Weapons (9 Weapons, 113-121)
113. Your cell phone and watch—put them away—and make sure TOS notices
114. Formalize your agreement with rituals and symbols
115. Prepare contract ahead of time and give it to TOS to sign
116. Be a rebel—buck the trend...be unpredictable
117. Never waste a crisis
118. *Turn* **my** *problem into* **our** *problem and finally into* **your** *problem (Over-used)*
119. Say *What if...?* And hope for a *How?* reply
120. Challenge TOS in order to inspire him
121. Be sure—use off-setting bets

92 Defensive Weapons
Subtle power (4 Weapons, 1-4)
1. *The power of powerlessness and creeping paralysis (Over-used)*
2. Ask for sympathy
3. Use TOS's sense of ethics, justice, and morality
4. *Remind TOS of his competition—real or imaginary (Over-used)*

Mind games (5 Weapons, 5-9)

5. **Distract TOS when he is overly aggressive, put him off-balance—Japanese-style (Under-used)**

6. *Use funny money, not real money (Over-used)*

7. Declare war on somebody else, not on TOS

8. Become an ostrich

9. **The person with the *least* commitment to the relationship has the *most* power (Under-used)**

Silence (3 Weapons, 10-12)

10. **Complete, total silence (Under-used)**

11. Don't react at all, neither positively nor negatively

12. Use the *pregnant pause*

The power of focusing on TOS (2 Weapons, 13-14)

13. Anticipate TOS's objections and defuse them in advance

14. *Keep TOS's expectations low (Over-used)*

Body language—the most important skill of influence and persuasion you'll ever learn (5 Weapons, 15-19)

15. **Watch TOS's body language very closely (Under-used)**

16. **Manipulate TOS with your own body language (Under-used)**

17. Use very reassuring body language

18. **Use touch power—the body language of touching (Under-used)**

19. **Use position power—the language spoken by office furniture (Under-used)**

Concessions (1 Weapon)

20. **Carefully observe the concession patterns of you and TOS—and keep a record of them (Under-used)**

Information (6 Weapons in 4 parts, 21-26)

Part 1. Get information (2 Weapons, 21-22)

21. Appear as harmless as TV's detective *Columbo*—then *zap!* TOS at the end

22.   Get and verify information—detect and expose bullshit

Part 2. Use information (1 Weapon)
23.   Assumptions—use them wisely

Part 3. Give information away (1 Weapon)
24.   **Grapevine gossip (Under-used)**

Part 4. Protect your information (2 Weapons, 25-26)
25.   Secure your secrets—adopt a fortress mentality
26.   Don't be a cheap amateur—use a professional security firm

<u>7 kinds of delays</u> (47 Weapons in 7 parts, 27-73)
Part 1. Obvious delays (5 Weapons, 27-31)
27.   Stall for time—get lost for a while
28.   Procrastinate openly
29.   *The power of being unprepared—forgetting on purpose (Over-used)*
30.   *Give TOS the run-around (Over-used)*
31.   Be overly bureaucratic

Part 2. My well is dry (4 Weapons, 32-35)
32.   *I can't afford it—I have no more money (Over-used)*
33.   I won't break the law
34.   My hands are tied—my company won't let me
35.   I won't go against my ethics

Part 3. Spin wheels—make TOS start all over again (4 Weapons, 36-39)
36.   New specifications
37.   New formal proposal
38.   Suggest different alternative
39.   Add new issues to written agendas

Part 4. Cloud, confuse, and complicate (7 Weapons, 40-46)
40.   Information overload—give TOS too much unimportant info full of minor details

41. Keep asking for more and more information
42. ***Don't give TOS very important information (Over-used)***
43. Extremely detailed explanation of unimportant matter
44. Insist on reading complicated stuff out loud
45. Keep talking so TOS can't talk
46. Extreme complication—set up a different organization structure, real or phony

Part 5. Transparent smokescreens (12 Weapons, 47-58)
47. **My dog ate my homework (Under-used)**
48. My dog ate my expert
49. ***Be honest—but only up to the point where it doesn't hurt you (Over-used)***
50. Suddenly have to go to the toilet
51. Suddenly get very hungry / thirsty
52. Give very poor explanation on purpose
53. Use *Creative Vagueness*
54. Change locations occasionally, not often
55. Replace your team's leader
56. Add team members who can slow things down
57. Spontaneous interruptions using a *Silent Buzzer*
58. **Get off the subject for a while—lighten up by using humor, talking about sports, etc. (Under-used)**

Part 6. Black holes (4 Weapons, 59-62)
59. Many investigations, one after the other
60. Set up fact-finding committee
61. Set up study group
52. Hold summit meeting

Part 7. Shields—protective defense mechanisms (11 Weapons, 63-73)
63. Ignore realities, concentrate on unrealistic possibilities instead
64. Avoid change by ignoring new information
65. Rationalizing
66. Over-identification with company
67. Take an ego trip—act like a VIP or big dog

68. Demand compensation when you're dissatisfied
69. Fluctuate between cheerfulness and mild anger
70. Project your faults onto TOS
71. ***Constant nagging—low-level negativity (Over-used)***
72. An overall and obviously strong attempt to dominate TOS
73. Act obnoxious and hostile

Using other people (5 Weapons, 74-78)
74. Teams overpower Lone Rangers
75. Join with others—lockouts, strikes, boycotts
76. **Find allies and use them (Under-used)**
77. Find *prestigious* allies and use them
78. Reposition TOS—make him not just your ally—make him your mentor

Using news media (3 Weapons, 79-81)
79. Get good publicity from news media
80. Even bad publicity can be good
81. Demonize TOS just for the publicity

What to do when TOS catches you doing something *naughty* (4 Weapons, 82-85)
82. Find a scapegoat
83. Say "Don't blame me, I didn't do it"
84. Say "Yeah, I did it, but the devil made me do it"
85. Admit your mistake and apologize before TOS tries to blame you

Defensive Weapons that are almost Assertive (7 Weapons, 86-92)
86. The worst case scenario
87. ***You gotta do better than that! (Over-used)***
88. ***Use trade-offs, but don't mess with promises (Over-used)***
89. Don't lose your momentum—don't give in to unreasonable demands
90. Debate, *no*; counterattack, *yes*
91. Make TOS pick the alternative *you* want
92. Make sure TOS has only one way out of danger—pleasing you

16 Submissive Weapons

<u>Conceding on both sides</u> (1 Weapon)

1. Put a dollar value on each concession you and TOS make

<u>Using time wisely</u> (2 Weapons, 2-3)

2. Buy time using promises
3. ***Drool and choose--give TOS several attractive choices that emotionally involve him (Over-used)***

<u>Word games</u> (2 Weapons, 4-5)

4. Say "Yes, *but*"
5. Say "Yes, *and*"—more effective

<u>Extreme Submission</u> (4 Weapons, 6-9)

6. Don't argue—turn the other cheek instead
7. Sponge, *yes*; wall, *no*
8. The nail that stands out gets hammered down
9. Beg—and if that doesn't work, pray

<u>Give in and save face at the same time</u> (3 Weapons, 10-12)

10. One step at a time
11. The contingent offer
12. The tough give-in—bargain harder each time you give up something

<u>Get help</u> (1 Weapon)

13. Last resort—use arbitration or mediation

<u>Submission by stupidity</u> (2 Weapons, 14-15)

14. ***Split the difference (Over-used)***
15. Self-destruction—*see* me, *catch* me, *stop* me, *save* me

<u>Submission by smarts</u> (1 Weapon)

16. ***Accept defeat and take what you can get—leave well enough alone (Over-used)***

24 Cooperative Weapons

The 3 essentials of Cooperation (3 Weapons, 1-3)

1. **Power of patience (Under-used)**
2. Make TOS happy—he'll become contented and committed to you
3. Consultant *yes*; sales rep, *no*

Form an alliance with TOS (4 Weapons, 4-7)

4. ***Reciprocity—you scratch my back, and I'll scratch yours (Over-used)***
5. Get the best ally of all—TOS himself
6. Intimacy—but no sex
7. Intimacy—with sex

Honesty (3 Weapons, 8-10)

8. Complete honesty—reveal your bottom line
9. Tell TOS your shortcomings— don't hide them
10. **Admit you don't know something—don't hide it (Under-used)**

Speaking (3 Weapons, 11-13)

11. Speak so clearly there's no chance TOS will misunderstand
12. Gain momentum—make it easy for TOS to say *yes* early and often
13. ***Make tempting promises instead of conceding (Over-used)***

Listening (2 Weapons, 14-15)

14. **The cheapest concession of all—listen, and listen well (Under-used)**
15. **Master *Active Listening* and use it often (Under-used)**

Keep cooperating even after the negotiation is over (4 Weapons, 16-19)

16. **The bonus—leave something extra on the table at the end (Under-used)**
17. When you win big, make sure TOS saves face
18. **Make sure TOS looks good at the end (Under-used)**
19. **Make TOS think you lost, even if you won big…think of the movie, *The Sting* (Under-used)**

5 degrees of cooperation (5 Weapons, 20-24)

20. **Mental seduction—become indispensable by *over*-cooperating (Under-used)**

21. Go *way* beyond what you *have* to do—send a limousine

22. Go only a *little* beyond what you *have* to do—send a bus ticket

23. Help TOS afford what you're offering

24. Ooze warmth, but try hard to appear sincere about it

81 Dirty Tricks

Timing (6 Weapons in 2 parts, 1-6)

Part 1. *Before* the negotiating begins (2 Weapons, 1-2)

1. **Make it impossible for TOS to go somewhere else at the last minute (Under-used)**

2. Get an invulnerable reputation--you brag, get others to brag about you

Part 2. *After* the negotiating is over (4 Weapons, 3-6)

3. **Sign contract, escalate immediately (Under-used)**

4. **Sign contract, re-negotiate immediately (Under-used)**

5. *Limited authority—but first, I have to ask my mommy (Over-used)*

6. Revenge—ruin TOS's victory celebration

Test TOS (2 Weapons, 7-8)

7. Deliberately break *minor* rules early

8. Deliberately make *minor* mistakes early

Deliberate incompetence (7 Weapons, 9-15)

9. Mix dates up on purpose

10. Confuse net and gross profit on purpose

11. Confuse simple and compound interest on purpose

12. Subtly change contract specifications on purpose and hope TOS doesn't notice

13. Something for nothing

14. Send TOS phony bill (small amount) on purpose

15. Buyer's bait-and-switch

Sneaky pricing (3 Weapons, 16-18)

16. **Seller's bait-and-switch (Under-used)**
17. Buyer's *very high* initial offer—the high-ball
18. Seller's *very low* initial offer, with protections—the low-ball

The law—using it and abusing it (4 Weapons, 19-22)

19. Frivolous lawsuit to harass TOS
20. Bribe TOS
21. Blackmail TOS
22. Extortion, shakedowns

Espionage (2 Weapons, 23-24)

23. Find out TOS's secrets legally
24. Find out TOS's secrets illegally

Arrogant attitude (3 Weapons, 25-27)

25. **Act untouchable—claim "I'm entitled to special privileges" (Under-used)**
26. Act *holier-than-thou*—use phony sanctimony
27. **Act smug—make TOS think you already know a lot about him and his company (Under-used)**

Words and rumors (3 Weapons, 28-30)

28. Smear TOS—guilt by alleged association
29. Isolate TOS—use the grapevine to spread bad rumors about TOS
30. Isolate your competitors—use the grapevine to spread bad rumors about them

Psychological warfare (19 Weapons, 31-48)

31. Humiliate and ridicule TOS
32. Make visitor face the sun—glare and stare
33. Chairs—yours, high; visitor's, low
34. Chairs—yours, stable; visitor's, wobbly
35. The steam bath—intentionally hot
36. The freezer—intentionally cold_
37. Your meeting room—intimidating décor

38. **Frightening ambience, manipulative music (Under-used)**
39. The marathon—all-night sessions
40. Keep TOS off-balance by frequently changing meeting time
41. The caterer from hell 1—really bad food and drink
42. The caterer from hell 2—mild food poisoning
43. Dirty visitor's toilet—the power of YUCK (You Use Contaminated Krapper)
44. Horrible smells in meeting room
45. Put visitors in The Roach Motel
46. Put visitors in The Twilight Zone
47. Many *planned* interruptions on purpose
48. Unusually pleasant interruptions

Real warfare (5 Weapons, 49-53)
49. Use the *Stockholm Syndrome*—create a bond with TOS, then exploit it
50. Act extremely hostile and nasty
51. ***Scare the hell out of TOS—make him fear you (Over-used)***
52. Irritate TOS—make him lose his temper
53. Actual violence—brute force

Dirty lies (3 Weapons, 54-56)
54. Double lying—back up your lies with misleading statistics
55. ***Obvious lying, not just exaggerated big talk (Over-used)***
56. Lie about withdrawing—you're still there, hiding behind intermediaries

Taking advantage of TOS's 2 G-Spots—gullibility and greed (19 Weapons in 4 parts, 57-75)
Part 1. Games buyers play on sellers (3 Weapons, 57-59)
57. Overbook on purpose—schedule several appointments at the same time
58. Guess who was here? Guess who's coming by later?
59. Guess who's in the next room?

Part 2. Games sellers play on buyers (2 Weapons, 60-61)

60. Extreme shortage
61. We'll soon drop this item

Part 3. Scam games (14 Weapons, 62-75)
Note: Watch out for them, but don't use them—they're unethical and illegal
2 Phishing scams (e-mail only) (2 Weapons, 62-63)
62. Lottery winner scams—contests, green cards
63. Nigerian scam—big bucks

3 Sympathy-seeking scams (3 Weapons, 64-66)
64. Magazine subscription at front door
65. Taxi money scam
66. Send me money at the airport

2 Crash-and-bump scams (2 Weapons, 67-68)
67. Minor car accident on purpose
68. Dead camel on the road to Dubai

2 Inspection scams (2 Weapons, 69-70)
69. Bribe me or I'll close you down for health violations
70. Inspector with secret partner fraud

3 Tourist scams (3 Weapons, 71-73)
71. Require deposit for phony service
72. Avoid customs duty fraud
73. Shakedown by phony cop

2 Sex scams (2 Weapons, 74-75)
74. Come meet my sister—she's a doctor
75. Sex party invitation

Part 4. The ultimate loser (1 Weapon)
76. ***The 2 G-spots: Take advantage of the ultimate loser's greed and gullibility (Over-used)***

<u>4 other Dirty Tricks</u> (4 Weapons, 77-80)

77. **Put TOS on the defensive—deliberately embarrass him, but only slightly (Under-used)**

78. Gross-out TOS by mildly disgusting behavior

79. Deliberate confusion: Adopt a name similar to a famous person, famous company

80. Dull TOS's senses and judgment—deliberately use drugs or alcohol to get him high or drunk

<u>The Dirtiest Trick of all</u> (1 Weapon)

81. Thick face, black heart

…plus one Weapon to use on whistle-blowers, terrorists, and emotionally-disturbed people: A special *leap year* Weapon against these kinds of people

Before telling you about Mao Tse-Tung's 22 most powerful guerrilla Weapons, here's something you guerrilla entrepreneurs may be interested in: Don's 365 tactics are the basis of his seminar, *How You Can Negotiate and Win*. He does this program mostly outside the U.S.—by choice. Why? Because almost all his clients are overseas. Please contact him if you would like to own a franchise to conduct this seminar in the U.S. and other parts of the world. He will do far more than coach you. He will train you and provide you with all seminar materials. Please go to **www.GuerrillaDon. com** for more information. Or e-mail Don at donhendon1@aol.com.

And if you use techniques that aren't in Don's list—winning techniques to get the other person to do what you want him to do—please send them to Don. He will include the strongest ones in a follow-up book and credit you for your submission. Thank you so much.

Mao Tse-Tung's 22 Most Powerful Guerrilla Weapons: List Prepared by Donald Wayne Hendon

Copyright (c) 2001-2012 by Dr. Donald Wayne Hendon

1. Always stay on the offensive.

2. Always stay alert so you'll see hidden opportunities to win.

3. Attack where the big dog is weakest.

4. Use shock and awe.

5. Ambush the big dog. Surprise him by attacking when and where he doesn't expect you to attack.

6. Know who to avoid and when to avoid him.

7. Attack only when your forces are superior.

8. Attack only when you're certain you'll win.

9. Be more mobile, more flexible than the big dog.

10. Lose your ego. Know when to withdraw. And do it, don't just think about it!

11. Retreat quickly whenever he becomes superior. Wait for another opportunity, then attack again.

12. Confuse the big dog by withdrawing quickly after you win a small victory.

13. Confuse him by spreading false information, too.

14. Put him off balance. When he thinks east, you attack from the west.

15. Take advantage of the big dog's rhythm when he is unsettled, and you'll win big.

16. Weaken him. How? Disperse him, harass him, exhaust him, disrupt his supply lines and his communication lines.

17. Use the big dog's supplies.

18. Get allies—you're an underdog, so you need help. Especially allies in his company and in the media.

19. Go one step beyond allies. Recruit spies—somebody in the big dog's company who holds a grudge against his bosses. He'll get his revenge by seeing you win.

20. Pay your spies well.

21. Don't trust your spies completely—they may be counterspies.

22. Be completely ruthless.

PART THREE

DONALD WAYNE HENDON'S 50 MOST POWERFUL AND *UNDER*-USED TACTICAL WEAPONS: GUERRILLAS SHOULD USE THEM BECAUSE THEY'RE POWERFUL AND BECAUSE THE BIG DOG WON'T EXPECT THEM—CHAPTERS 5-9

Most big dogs probably won't expect you to use these Weapons, because they are so rare. And, of course, that's a big reason why they're extremely powerful. If you're a *real* guerrilla, someone who thinks outside the conventional box, you'll fall in love with them and use them often on both big dogs and guerrillas. But what happens when you try to make a deal with another guerrilla? Even though you'll probably be dealing more with big dogs than with other guerrillas, you'll often run into guerrillas in your business and personal life. Be prepared—use the winning counter-punches you find in Chapters Five to Nine. They work well on other guerrillas as well as on big dogs.

Chapter Five discusses eight of Don's 50 most powerful and under-used tactical Weapons. They're in the Preparation category. And here's what's in Chapters Six through Nine:

- Chapter Six covers 14 Assertive Weapons.
- Chapter Seven talks about 12 Defensive Weapons.
- There are no powerful under-used Submissive Weapons, so Chapter Eight goes into eight Cooperative Weapons.
- Chapter Nine covers eight Dirty Tricks.

Let's get started with the eight most powerful and under-used Preparation Weapons in Chapter Five.

CHAPTER 5

EIGHT PREPARATION WEAPONS—
POWERFUL AND *UNDER*-USED

What this chapter is all about: Eight Preparation Weapons—learn
from children, the right attitude, don't give away the store for a
smile, mistakes, escalation, thinking small, be hungry, and when
to make deals.

Before you guerrillas can start the deal-making process, you've got to prepare
yourself by adopting the right mental attitude and by getting information. You
need info about both the situation and the big dog or other guerrilla you're
going to negotiate with. Here are the eight most powerful—and *under*-used—
tactical Weapons to use to prepare yourself to be a winner in dealing with
anybody, both big dogs and other guerrillas. Since they're not used very often,
the person on the other side of the table from you will be surprised when
you use them—and that gives you a *big* advantage! Chapter Four listed all of
Don's 31 Preparation Weapons. These under-used eight Weapons are the most
powerful of the 31.

Preparation Weapon 4: Overcome the Paralysis of Not Thinking Fast Enough by Learning from Children

Thinking on your feet gives you a big advantage over big dogs. Most of them will use old, tired playbooks that stick to strict rules and procedures. The best guerrillas are imaginative, creative, innovative, and can think on their feet and adapt quickly. Easy to say, hard to do. Or *is* it? Here's one fast and simple way to get there: Become more like the child you used to be. *Because children are natural guerrillas!*

Children are bursting with life, can go off in many different ways, have lots of energy, have lots of strategies and tactics in reserve—even if they don't know they do. Above all, they sense that even if they fail, they can still come back with a new and better idea. Compare children to adults. Adults feel bound by rules on all sides, are unable to maneuver, and are afraid to take risks. An adult is like a crude computer game with limited memory and limited processor capability. When you play a computer game with a child, who usually wins, who is more powerful? You know the answer: The child. Become more like a child. Become a winner!

Becoming more like children is especially important for guerrillas. Look at this box which shows the difference between adults and children:

Adults live by these rules	Children violate these rules because they believe that
There's a right way and a wrong way	There are many different ways to do something
Don't ask stupid questions	Asking stupid questions can give us new insights
Experts are always right	Experts are often wrong
Don't be silly	Being silly liberates you from the pressures of conformity
Don't make a mistake	Mistakes sometimes lead to brilliant insights, great discoveries
Don't play with that	Everything is a toy to children because they have the extraordinary capability to turn common objects into play things. Imagination: Everything has the potential to become something else

Now, substitute *Big Dog* for *Adults* and *Guerrillas* for *Children*. See what we mean?

Two Winning Guerrilla Counter-Punches

If you feel threatened by creative people, you're probably not very creative yourself. Fortunately, there are ways to become more creative, even if you're set in your ways and don't like to try new things.

> Don often gives a seminar on how to be more creative. Here are 11 of the most important techniques he talks about:
>
> * Become more like a child
> * Brainstorming
> * Attribute-listing
> * Structural analysis
> * Forced relationships
> * Suspend judgment
> * Lateral thinking
> * The bug list
> * 101 uses
> * Brain aerobics
> * Read books on how to be more creative and perform the exercises in them
>
> Please go to **www.GuerrillaDon.com** to get a report explaining these 11 techniques in detail.

If the guy on the other side of the table is being overly child-like, it's best not to let it bother you. Let him continue to have fun. He might even entertain you. However, if he goes off on a tangent too often and if this bothers you, here are two winning guerrilla counter-punches you can try to get him to act more like an adult:

* First, try Assertive Weapon 112, *Threaten doomsday*. That is, predict disaster for the big dog unless he accepts your offer. But make sure your prediction is likely to occur.

- This next counter-punch isn't as powerful as *Doomsday*, because many of you don't have this power and it's hard to get. It's *Intimidating the big dog by using lawful, legitimate power* (Assertive 86). This is the kind of power a policeman has. Thinking you have *right* on your side may blind you into thinking you have this kind of power—but if the big dog doesn't think you have this power, then you really have no power at all.

Preparation Weapon 5: The Right Attitude—I've Got to Earn the Right to Learn the Other Guy's Needs

Before you can earn the right to learn the other guy's needs, you've got to be comfortable with ambiguity and uncertainty. Remember when you were learning to ride a bicycle? Think of that when you're trying to close a deal. The deal-making process is chaotic, not predictable, stable, linear. Deal-making, like life, is all about *balancing*, not about *being balanced*. Don't use the wobble as a crutch, as an excuse. *Embrace the wobble*, because in the art of balancing, moving from security to insecurity and back again, you come alive. So develop a tolerance for insecurity. Don't drive yourself crazy by trying to know everything about the big dog simply because you want to control everything. You're a guerrilla, after all, and you'll never be as powerful as the big dog, not even after you beat him.

One Winning Guerrilla Counter-Punch

If the big dog is being too ambiguous, try Cooperative Weapon 3: *Consultant, yes; sales rep, no*. Remember, the other person's needs are among his most important possessions. He guards them because they contain the secrets to his future success. You already know your own needs, especially your need to get the big dog to do what you want him to do, and so you don't have to concentrate on them. Concentrate instead on learning *his* needs. When you know what they are, you'll be able to come up with a plan to satisfy them—with your products and services.

But don't go crazy trying to learn *all* his needs. Think about your spouse, the person closest to you in the whole world. Do you know all of her needs? Definitely not! She won't tell you some of them, even though she loves you. So don't expect the big dog to tell you all his needs, either.

How do you earn the right to learn the big dog's needs? Not just by asking questions and listening well. You do this by acting as a consultant—not as a persuader, a sales rep, a manipulator When you're trying to persuade him, you're concentrating on *your own* needs to make a sale—not on *his* needs. Consultants concentrate on the other guy's needs. It may take you a long time to gain his confidence, but it will pay big dividends when you do.

Don't take this too far, though. A consultant isn't the same thing as a chameleon. Chameleons adapt *too much* to match the other person. Keep your identity, keep your integrity (Preparation 18).

Preparation Weapon 8: Don't Give Away the Store Just to See the Big Dog Smile

Don't give the big dog too much just so he'll like you. You should like yourself so much that you won't have that much of a need to be liked by him. Replace the saying, *No money, no honey*, with *Money can't buy me love*.

What's so bad about being afraid of being disliked? This fear makes you give more stuff away. Let's say you're the department head and you don't discipline employees who take two hour lunch breaks all the time because you want to be "nice." Not only will these bums show their contempt of you by continuing to take their long lunch hours, but eventually they won't pay attention to other parts of their job. Other employees in your department will notice this. And instead of being liked, you become the object of contempt. You lose everybody's respect. And your department's productivity goes way, way down.

Three Winning Guerrilla Counter-Punches
If the big dog doesn't care if you like him or not, then he probably has more business than he can handle. He thinks he doesn't need your business. Here are three things you can do about it:

- *Get and verify information* by doing your homework. Find out how successful he really is (Defensive 22).
- Then, use what you found out to make him think two things: That getting your business will make him even more successful than he is now. And that he's in danger of losing it (Assertive 39, *I'm the greatest.* Defensive 88, *Reward-punishment*).

- When you tell him all this, massage his ego—flatter him. Big dogs usually have big egos, and they love to be flattered (Assertive 60, *Smooth talk, flattery, and charm*. Cooperative 24, *Ooze warmth*).

Preparation Weapon 11: Mistakes— Admit Them, Learn from Them

Liking yourself helps your ego. But when you use Weapon 11, you've got to forget about your ego. When you put your ego on hold, as Preparation Weapon 10 suggests, it's easier for you to make a list of your mistakes. We suggest you make a list, keep it updated, and learn from your mistakes. Try to avoid making them again.

Actually, it's easier than you think to make a list. Two reasons:

First, it's fun to read or hear about stupid things other people did. Like stupid convenience store robbers. One of Don's books, *Classic Failures in Product Marketing*, has more than 800 business mistakes in 68 categories. Many of them are just plain stupid—and funny. Go to **www.GuerrillaDon. com** for information on how to get this out-of-print book from Don— autographed, too.

Second, we remember our pain more than our happiness. Pain is rare. It hurts a lot. We seek happiness, and many things make us happy. None stand out that much. Pain, however, stands out.

But even though we remember our painful mistakes, we often repeat them. Why? Because failure is personal and emotional. When you fail, your anxiety levels skyrocket. At times, you even deny you failed. You talk about *errors* and *mistakes* instead—anything except that dreaded word, *failure*. And you use euphemisms: *Gone to his reward* instead of *death*. *Lady of the night* for *whore*. And *rapid oxidation* when a nuclear reactor suffers a serious partial meltdown. When this happened in Pennsylvania, the press release said the damaged reactor core emitted no more heat than *17 home toasters*.

Don't use euphemisms. Call them *mistakes*, because that's what they are. Acknowledge them, learn from them, and don't make them again!

Two Winning Guerrilla Counter-Punches

- Don't get upset when the big dog reminds you of your mistakes. Instead, thank him for telling you (Preparation 10, *Deal with your ego*).

- If you know the big dog pretty well and have a good relationship with him, tell him in a *just kidding* manner when he makes a certain mistake. Make him think you'll help him avoid these kinds of mistakes in the future. When he thinks of you as a mentor, you become one of his most valuable customers (Defensive 78, *Reposition TOS—make him not just your ally—make him your mentor*). (Please remember TOS stands for the other side.) Do all you can to make him lose his ego.

Preparation Weapon 13: The Escalation Commitment: Throwing Good Money After Bad Is Just Plain Stupid

If you're already in a hole, stop digging! You'll only make it bigger! Staying at the deal-making table even after you have lost a lot, making more and more concessions is stupid. This is very powerful—but not for the person who *does* it. It's very powerful for the person who's *on the receiving end*. Here's what we mean:

Emotions, positive and negative, mess up everybody's decision-making process, guerrillas and big dogs alike. Sellers should look for customers who stay in play a long time after they should have gotten out. They're gold mines, making one concession after another!

If you tend to do this, you're a loser. Here are five things you can do about it:

- Lose your ego. Be cold and calculating, like chess players (Preparation 30, *Learn and master chess*). Chess isn't a clean, intellectual engagement. Former world champion Garry Kasparov said, "It's a violent sport, and when you confront your opponent, you set out to crush his ego." Chess is a battleground on which the enemy has to be vanquished. Never be too emotional. Emotional people are losers, in our opinion—they do stupid things simply to justify a bad decision they made earlier.
- Learn from poker players, too. It's easy to spot losers at a card table—even after they've bet a large amount of money, they keep calling further bets even when it's clear they can't win the pot. Their emotions tell them that the money they've already put in the pot belongs to them. They forget that the money they've already bet has nothing to do with whether they should continue playing a hand or not. They don't know when to hold 'em, don't know when to fold 'em.

- This applies to your relationship with your lover. Many people in dead-end relationships have invested several years in that relationship. They can't admit to themselves they made a mistake. Many go ahead and get married anyway. But these marriages often end in divorce. They're doing the same thing bad poker players do—throwing good money after bad. So when things get too bad, get out, and get out quickly. Cut your losses. Hanging on is for losers! Thank goodness you're a guerrilla. Remember, guerrillas have *a lot less* to lose than big dogs.

- Carry a pen, paper, and calculator. Keep them in front of you at all times when you're negotiating. Concentrate on the numbers, not on your emotions (Assertive 54, *Control the agreement process itself*).

- Try your best not to make decisions until after your emotions subside (Defensive 28, *Procrastinate openly*). How long will this take? Your emotional turmoil lasts a long time after a death in the family or a divorce. It lasts only a short time when the guy in the car in front of you cuts you off. The length of time for you will be somewhere in between these two extremes.

Winning Guerrilla Counter-Punches—Zero

Preparation 13 is under-used and very powerful—powerful for the person on the other side, that is! So there's absolutely no counter-punches here! The guy on the other side of the table is a goldmine! Mine the gold! Try to make deals with stupid people—big dogs and guerrillas alike—who keep throwing good money after bad. Take advantage of their stupidity. On the other hand, if you want to make the big dog feel you have his best interests at heart, offer to postpone negotiations with him when he's feeling sad (Cooperative 2, *Make TOS happy—he'll become contented and committed to you*). He'll think of you as more noble, caring, and wise.

Preparation Weapon 16: Think Small

We think you should adopt this as your overall guiding philosophy. Why? Because this is *the* quintessential guerrilla Weapon. It's what makes a guerrilla a guerrilla. In Chapter Two, we talked about Sam Walton, the most successful business guerrilla of all time. He thought small and won big. Always remember this—smaller companies have less to lose, so they feel they can do *anything*.

Big dog companies have more to lose if they make a mistake, so they usually don't take quick action. Fear of big losses paralyzes them, so they miss opportunities that guerrillas take advantage of. As a popular song of the 1970s said, "Freedom's just another word for nothing left to lose." (From *Me and Bobby McGee*.)

Set Yourself Free—Get Big by Thinking Small! is the title of one of Don's forthcoming books. Watch for it. More details are at **www.GuerrillaDon.com**

Two Winning Guerrilla Counter-Punches
- Your entire book is about thinking small, of thinking like a guerrilla, of winning like guerrillas win. You've got a lot of Weapons to choose from. So when you're trying to make a deal with another guerrilla, you should *think small* too (Preparation 16). Big dogs probably will never use this Weapon—it goes against their very nature.
- In the meantime, remembering Sam Walton's way of winning will make you feel better about being a guerrilla. Take chances. *Dare to fail* (Preparation 14). You'll lose your fear of dealing with big dogs. You might even want to hang Sam's picture in your office and even carry his picture in your wallet. They'll remind you how you can be a big winner like Wal-Mart's founder. Take pride in your guerrilla-ness.

Preparation Weapon 26: Negotiate on an Empty Stomach
Why? Because physical hunger leads to psychological hunger. When most people hear about this for the first time, they don't believe it. Many of Don's clients didn't believe it until they tried it. They soon realized it works wonders. So when you're physically hungry, when you hear your stomach growling, you're hungry psychologically as well. You'll want more, and you'll ask for more. Bottom line: You'll get more. And when you have a full stomach, you're probably somewhat sleepy and not very alert. More importantly, you'll be full psychologically as well, and you won't ask for very much. Bottom line: You'll get less.

Two Winning Guerrilla Counter-Punches
- Try not to negotiate on a full stomach. And watch out if you hear the big dog's stomach growling (*Listen well*, Cooperative 14). He's hungry and he'll probably want more from you.

- If you think he's hungry, do all you can to delay the deal-making session till after lunch. He'll appreciate your thoughtfulness (Defensive 27, *Stall for time—get lost for a while*).

Preparation Weapon 27: Make Deals in the Morning, Not in the Afternoon

This is another Weapon that most people don't believe the first time they hear about it. But it works. Big dogs and guerrillas who work normal business hours, 8 or 9 a.m. to 5 p.m., are more alert in the mornings. By mid-afternoon, they're tired. So we think the best time to make deals is at 10 a.m. when you're alert, and the worst time is around 2:30 p.m. when you're tired. The marketers of the drink, Five-Hour Energy Shot, seem to agree with us. Their ads stress that office workers feel most sluggish, tired, and lazy around 2:30 p.m.

One Winning Guerrilla Counter-Punch

Even if you think you're a night person, it's still better to negotiate in the morning. If the big dog or other guerrilla demands an afternoon session, you might want to consume an energy drink about an hour before talks begin (Preparation 25, *Be in good physical condition*).

There's another way this Weapon can be used. If the big dog visits you in your office, offer him coffee, not orange juice. Why? An experiment, reported in a scholarly journal, came up with these results: He agrees with you more often when you serve him coffee (not de-caf coffee) than when you serve him orange juice—35 percent more often, in fact. Coffee makes us more alert

Don't Run Away from Scholarly Journals—They're Powerful!

We'll bet a lot of you were turned off when we mentioned *scholarly journal*. Although we're both guerrillas and have been for a long time, we've gotten a lot of great insights from reading journals aimed at university professors and researchers. We suggest you look at some of them from time to time. Go online and check out the titles of articles. Read the articles you think will help you. We think the six scholarly journals with the best articles on how to get other people to do what you want them to do are these:

- Journal of Personality and Social Psychology
- Journal of Applied Social Psychology

- Journal of Applied Psychology
- Journal of Experimental Psychology
- Journal of Consumer Psychology
- Journal of Consumer Research

CHAPTER 6

14 ASSERTIVE WEAPONS— POWERFUL AND *UNDER*-USED

What this chapter is all about: Sudden moves, turning liabilities into assets, wild and crazy actions, make buyers pursue you, rule of three, make big dog invest time, powerful knowledge, using assistants, implying power, scare-and-rescue, swarming ambush, taking versus talking, untouchables, and deaf ear.

Chapter Four lists all 121 Assertive Weapons. Both Jay and Don like Assertive Weapons more than those in any other group because they seem to work best for us. Perhaps these Weapons suit our guerrilla personalities.

What is a *guerrilla personality*? Assertiveness/aggressiveness is definitely a very important guerrilla characteristic. Dr. Peter Hurd, a university professor in Canada, has published several studies on, of all things, the length of a person's finger and how aggressive or passive that person is. People whose index fingers are much shorter than their ring fingers are much more aggressive than people whose index and ring fingers are the same length. This has to do with the amount of testosterone in your mother's womb. Other researchers have looked into finger lengths and homosexuality. (We'll bet you're looking at your fingers right now!)

Or perhaps it's because of what many of the participants in Don's persuasion-influence-power-negotiating seminars tell him—the same thing, all over the world, year in and year out: If you start out with an aggressive opening bid and give ground only reluctantly, letting the person you're dealing with know it hurts you to make a concession—you'll get more (Submissive Weapon 12, *The tough give-in*). Big dogs and guerrillas alike agree on this. Many studies we've seen over the years have backed us up. Here's one from 2007:

- People with aggressive opening bids got *much* more than people whose opening bids were more "reasonable."
- Buyers with weak opening bids paid a lot more than sellers were willing to accept.
- Sellers with weak opening bids got a lot less than buyers were willing to offer.
- The weird thing was that each side felt it got the better end of the negotiation, probably because each side was never able to estimate the other's bottom line accurately. Apparently, ignorance is bliss.

We also don't use Defensive Weapons that much because 18 bad things can happen to people who are overly defensive. And because 20 good things happen to people when they stop their defensiveness. For details about this, including 20 reasons why people become defensive in the first place, please go to **www.GuerrillaDon.com**.

Now, here are Don's 14 most powerful under-used Assertive Weapons:

Assertive Weapon 1: Make Sudden, Unexpected Moves

Putting big dogs and other guerrillas off-balance will often make them change their plans to your advantage. Japan's greatest Samurai warrior, Miyamoto Musashi, who lived in the late 1500s and early 1600s, wrote *Go Rin No Sho: The Book of Five Rings*, after he retired from service to his emperor. It's been reprinted many times. One of his most important recommendations is to maintain your balance and at the same time distract your enemies and put them off-balance. Yes, he was the one who first said, "Take advantage of their rhythm when they're unsettled, and you'll win." You'll come across *Go Rin No Sho* again when you read Defensive Weapon 5 in Chapter Seven.

There are many ways to do this. Here's one way Don has seen often used by Indian shopkeepers in malls throughout Asia. They yell "Excuse me, excuse me" to people passing by their small shop. The startled passers-by then get a sales pitch from the merchant. Don usually responds by asking them, "What? Are my shoes on fire?" Then, he gives them a disgusted look and keeps on walking.

Here's another way. Let's say you're selling Christmas cards door-to-door. Which one of these three sales pitches do you think work best? (1) The cost is only 345 cents—a bargain! (2) The cost is only $3.45—a bargain! (3) The cost is only $3.45.

Answer: The first sales pitch beat the second sales pitch by two-to-one. The third sales pitch got mediocre results, because it didn't say $3.45 was a bargain. Why? *345 cents* is unexpected. Guerrillas do the unexpected.

Three Winning Guerrilla Counter-Punches
- Don't let the big dog distract you from your goal—to win big from him (Preparation 17, *Commit yourself totally*).
- But be nice—don't use sarcasm like Don does when Indian shopkeepers try to distract him. Use Cooperative 24 (*Ooze warmth*), and avoid Assertive 2 (*Attack TOS's ego—abuse by sarcasm*). Please remember, TOS stands for the other side.
- Sometimes, the big dog will try to distract you by bringing up something else. For example, let's say you're trying to get one of your employees to stop arriving late at work. If he says, "Other employees come into work late, and you don't say anything to them." Here's how to handle this: Distract him and put him on the defensive by asking him questions such as "If I let you come to work late but I don't let other employees do this, people will think I'm playing favorites with you. Is that what you want—to be known as the boss's pet?" This is Defensive 5, *Distract and put him off-balance Japanese-style*.

Assertive Weapon 17: Turn Your Liabilities into Assets—then *Zap!* the Other Guy at the End

First impressions are often wrong, but they're lasting. For example, let's say you're short, fat, have a dumb-looking face, and your voice is squeaky. If you're nerd-like, take advantage of it. Sure, your physical limitations make a bad first impression on people, but this makes them underestimate you. In fact, we recommend that you play along with it by your subsequent actions. Why? To make big dogs and other guerrillas underestimate you even more. Then, at the right time, *zap* them—prove to them by your use of deal-making skills and other actions that you are knowledgeable, skillful, and talented. This will surprise the big dog or other guerrilla you're dealing with, and surprise him in a very favorable way.

Two Winning Guerrilla Counter-Punches

Watch out for nerdy-type people. They may try for that nerdy look on purpose so you'll underestimate them. Many of these nerds will probably surprise you, and that will cost you money.

- So get as much information about them as possible before your deal-making gets really serious (Defensive 22, *Get and verify information*).
- And pre-empt them by letting them know how much you know about them (Dirty Trick 27, *Act smug—make TOS think you already know a lot about him and his company*).

Assertive Weapon 18: Put on a Good Show by Acting Wild and Crazy

Put on a good act—the wilder and crazier, the better. When you show big dogs and other guerrillas how emotionally committed you are to your position, your credibility goes way up. This gives them a good reason to settle on *your* terms. How wild and crazy should you be? As we said in Chapter Five, learn from children. Imitate these natural guerrillas. Try using temper tantrums, violating rules, acting cute, crying, acting strangely and weirdly, and so forth. We talked about this in Preparation Weapon 4—remember?

Four Winning Guerrilla Counter-Punches

Try these four counter-punches when big dogs or other guerrillas pull this act on you:

- Watch everything in silence. Keep silent even after the big dog stops his weird behavior. Shake your head disapprovingly. Then, after about ten more seconds of silence, tell him, "Glad you got that out of your system. Now, shall we get down to business?" Make sure you don't sound sarcastic, though. Use Defensive 10 (*Complete, total silence*). Avoid Assertive 2 (*Attack TOS's ego—abuse by sarcasm*).

- Every time he acts this way, withdraw your previous offer. Eventually, he'll realize his bad behavior is costing him money (Preparation 19, *How to make concessions—20 do's and 20 don'ts*).

- Tell him "I love watching you. You show such emotion and passion when you put on your act. You must really love what you do." Use Assertive 52 (*Confront TOS—ask "Why are you using Dirty Tricks, and when will you stop?"*) and Assertive 60, (*Smooth talk, flattery, and charm.*)

- If his behavior *really* upsets you and if his business isn't worth that much to you, just walk out. Life's too short to put up with this kind of garbage (Assertive 68).

Assertive Weapon 20: For Sellers: Make Buyers Pursue You for a Change

Instead of trying to sell the big dog buyer on how desirable your offer is, put him on the defensive—make him prove why he deserves what you're offering him. Don't be presumptuous or arrogant, though. This isn't very logical, but it's very effective. Here's an example: You're applying for a job. Tell the big dog interviewer, "I've already got two job offers. Please tell me why I should work for you and not for one of the other two companies?"

Three Winning Guerrilla Counter-Punches

- Ask the big dog buyer for specific numbers (Defensive 22, *Get and verify information*). Tell him you need this information so you'll know if you can match them or beat them.

- And if he won't give you this information, just walk away (Assertive 68, *Elvis has left the building*).

- Finally, let him know that you're evaluating him along with other prospects. This gives you extra leverage. Use that leverage to counterbalance the defensiveness he's been trying to make you feel. And make sure he knows that if he loses your account, he loses a lot (Assertive 39, *I'm the greatest*).

Assertive Weapon 25: A Chinese Favorite—the Rule of Three

Although this Weapon is used all over the world, it seems to be a special favorite of Chinese. Here's what it means: Say *no* to the big dog's first two offers--automatically. Don't say *yes* until after he makes his third offer. Think about it: If you're an *eager beaver* and accept the first offer the big dog or another guerrilla makes (ignoring Assertive 24), you'll probably either think one of two things: You paid too much. Or something's wrong with what you just bought. Saying *yes* too early makes you a victim of *the winner's curse*, and eventually you'll probably try to get out of the deal. Furthermore, the big dog will have contempt for you, because he expects you to be smart enough to play the game, to negotiate. He won't respect dumb people. And saying *yes* too early makes you look dumb.

You should try the rule of three on big dogs and other guerrillas. We'll bet they won't say *yes* until your third offer—if offer number three is somewhat close to what they want from you. It's good not to violate this psychologically powerful rule. The other person—whether he's a big dog or another guerrilla— will feel better after giving you two *no's*.

Three Winning Guerrilla Counter-Punches

- Don't be over-eager to make a sale. Remember if he says *no*, the big dog is just trying to make sure you know he's not the over-eager one. So when he says *no* to you, don't immediately come up with an over-generous counter-offer (Preparation 19, *Concessions: 20 do's and 20 don'ts*). Remember, both of you are just playing according to the rules of the game.
- What's a good way to say *no*? Try this: "Your offer sounds OK to me, but I've got to talk it over with my boss first." Of course, this is Dirty Trick 5 (*Limited authority—but first, I've got to ask my mommy*).
- Another good way: Tell him "*You gotta do better than that*" (Defensive 87).

Assertive Weapon 27: Learn from Car Dealers—
Make Big Dogs and Guerrillas Invest a Lot of Their Time

When big dogs or guerrillas put more time into any venture, they become more committed to the outcome. And so whenever you get somebody to invest a *lot* of time in dealing with you, you'll improve your chances of getting the deal you want. But, as Preparation Weapon 2 says, *pick your battles carefully*. Your time is invested, too, so do this *only* if *your* time is worth less to you than *their* time is worth to them. So before you even think about using this powerful Weapon, figure out in dollars how much your time is worth and try to guess what the big dog's time is worth to him. Here's how to do it:

The Dollar Value of Each Hour

Divide your total income from last year by 2,000. (Why 2,000? That's how many hours you probably worked last year—assuming 40 hours a week, 50 weeks a year, two weeks' vacation. If you worked more or less, use that figure instead of 2,000.) That's how much money you made each working hour last year. Let's assume you earned $400,000 last year. Divide that by 2,000, and you made $200 each hour. If you and the big dog are $1,000 apart, it makes sense to haggle for another hour, because if you get the entire $1,000 from him, you made an extra $800 profit. But be realistic. How many hours of haggling will it take to get the entire $1,000 extra from him? Don't bother haggling if you think it will take five hours or more. Just accept his offer. For more information on time management in deal-making, please go to **www.GuerrillaDon.com**.

Car dealers are natural big dogs or big dog wanna-be's, and they do this a lot. They figure, "The longer this guy stays in the showroom, the more likely he'll buy a car." Don's 11,000-word story about how he outwitted a hard-sell car dealer with a gong in its showroom is at **www.DonaldHendon.com**. Download it there, not at **www.GuerrillaDon.com**. It also appears in his *365 Powerful Ways to Influence* book. He's now writing a book about how to outwit car dealers. Probable title: *Never Buy a Car from a Dealer with a Gong in the Showroom*. Why a gong in the showroom? Every time a salesman sold a car, he rang the bell. This generated lots of enthusiasm among the salesmen, but it left a bad taste in most of the mouths of buyers and prospective buyers. If you see a gong in the showroom, get out quickly!

Seven Winning Guerrilla Counter-Punches
- *Make the big dog invest a lot of his time*, too (Assertive 27). Chances are, his time is more valuable to him than yours is to you—remember, you're

the guerrilla and have less to lose. And this gives you an advantage. If the big dog invests a lot of his time in the deal, he'll probably do more to make sure you're happy and the deal goes through.

Here are three ways to get both big dogs and guerrillas to invest a lot of their time:

- Get them to make a special visit to your company to tour your facilities. This gives you a great opportunity to show off (Assertive 39, *I'm the greatest*).
- Give them a list of your satisfied customers. Do all you can to make them contact your customers to get more information about you and your company (Cooperative 8, *Complete honesty*).
- Ask them a lot of questions about their products and services. And get them to explain their answers in detail (Defensive 22, *Get and verify information*).

And if the big dog tricks you into investing a lot of your time and then offers you a lot less than you thought you were going to get, here are three things you can do:
- *Confront TOS--call his bluff* (Assertive 51). Tell him directly, "I can't accept what you're offering." Here are two ways to prove you can't accept his offer:
- *I can't afford it—no money* (Defensive 32).
- Company policy won't let me do what you want (Defensive 31, *Be overly bureaucratic*).

Assertive Weapon 32: Know Your Enemy and Know Yourself—Knowledge Is Power

Around 8,000 years ago, Chinese general, Sun Tzu said "Know your enemy and know yourself, and you'll win every battle." We wouldn't go that far. Not *every* battle. We *will* say this, though: The big dog isn't your enemy. You need him and he needs you. Knowledge gives you a lot of power. And so knowing the strong points of the big dog and yourself will help you win more often.

Guerrillas should read the many translations available of Sun Tzu's *The Art of War*. There are many gems in it, such as "Keep your friends close and your enemies closer." Big dogs will get a lot out of it, too. It helps them understand how guerrillas think and act.

Don't forget about knowing yourself, too. Get rid of your *blind spots* (Preparation 9). You probably have a lot of them. All people do.

Five Winning Guerrilla Counter-Punches

- Keep control over the information you give the big dog (Assertive Weapon 55, *Limit what your team can tell TOS*).
- Using the *grapevine* (Defensive 24) to leak information to him is very powerful. But you have less control here, and this may be dangerous—he may get the wrong impression.
- If you don't want to risk using the grapevine, launch a trial balloon instead (Assertive 119). *Say "What if...?"* You're on your way to making a sale when the big dog replies, *"How?"*
- Don't forget to find out what he knows about you (Defensive 22, *Get and verify information*).
- A good way to find this out is to develop sources within the big dog's organization. Become friendly with them (Cooperative 5, *Get the best ally of all—TOS himself*).

Assertive Weapon 36: Turn the Big Dog's Top Assistants into Heroes

Learn as much as you can about the big dog's closest assistants and what they do. Many of them are technical experts. Talk to your own technical experts. Use them to convince the big dog's assistants that accepting your offer is the best thing for their boss to do. Get them so ego-involved in your project that they'll recommend accepting your offer to their boss. They are now your *allies* (Cooperative 5 again). And they'll help you win big.

Three Winning Guerrilla Counter-Punches

Here's what you can do when the big dog infiltrates your company and tries to get your assistants to recommend that you should accept his offer:

- Check your assistants' loyalty to you. Watch them to see if they've changed their attitudes toward the big dog. If so, try and find out why.

Do something about it if it's to your advantage (Defensive 22, *Get and verify information*).

- If necessary, impose communication limits so your assistants don't give important information to the big dog (Assertive 55, *Limit what your team can tell TOS*).
- Get your own ally, someone who will say good things about you to the big dog. This person can be in or outside his company (Defensive 76, *Find allies and use them*).

Assertive Weapon 41: *Imply* Your power—Don't Intentionally *Display* It

Don't try to overpower the big dog. He knows he's more powerful. Instead, you should *imply* you're powerful. Here are six ways to do this:

- Use words that imply action and authority instead of less specific words. For example, "I recommend" instead of "I think."
- The cleaner you look and smell, the more powerful you appear to be.
- If you're a male, wear an expensive black or dark blue coat and bright red necktie. For some reason, clothing coaches say red and black is a good power combination.
- Put one hand in the pocket of your coat, and let your thumb stick out. Showing the thumb is a subtle indicator of power.
- Another subtle indicator of power is simply raising an eyebrow to express disapproval or disbelief. Doing this is much more effective than yelling and screaming. If you yell at your employees, it will work only for a short time. If you keep it up, it becomes the norm, and your employees will soon ignore you.
- Take as little as possible with you to the meeting. The least powerful person—the secretary—carries the most stuff to the meeting. The person with the most power doesn't need to carry anything, because he has the power to make the final decision.

There's more information about how to subtly overpower your opponent in Chapter 16's section, The Body Language of Dominance. You'll find 18 gestures indicating dominance there.

Four Winning Guerrilla Counter-Punches

Here's what to do when the big dog tries a subtle power play on you:

- Be smart enough and alert enough to recognize what the big dog's doing (Assertive 32, *Know TOS and know yourself—knowledge is power*).
- Don't feel threatened. Don't let his power displays affect you—even if they are subdued displays (Assertive 70, *Be brave, not scared*).
- Should you mimic him and do the same things he does? If you decide to do this, learn as much as you can about power. Check out the 95 factors in Don's *Prism of Power*. It's online at **www.GuerrillaDon. com**. You can also find a shorter version in Chapter 19 of his *365 Powerful Ways to Influence* book.

Here's what *not* to do: Don't get into an obvious pissing contest with him. Instead, do some of the things he's doing, but do them even more subtly (Defensive 16, *Manipulate TOS with your own body language*).

Assertive Weapon 45: Scare the Big Dog, Then Rescue Him

Do your homework. Find out what problems the other guy has. Scare him by telling him about the terrible things that might happen if he doesn't solve his problems. Then, let him know you can rescue him with your product or service. This is difficult to do successfully. You've got to show a lot of sincerity here (Cooperative Weapons 8 and 24—*Complete honesty* and *Ooze warmth*). If you don't, he won't believe you. The upside: This works on both big dogs and guerrillas.

Four Winning Guerrilla Counter-Punches

Try one or more of these four counter-punches. All of them have worked for us.

- Say, "Who, me? Sorry I didn't know." You've got to be a good actor, though, or it won't work (Assertive 11, *Playing dumb is smart*).
- *Don't react all, either positively or negatively* (Defensive 11).
- Do the same thing the big dog is trying to do to you—*scare him, then come to his rescue* (Assertive 45).

- Act like you're *invulnerable*, that nothing can hurt you (Dirty Trick 2, *You brag, get others to brag about you*).

Assertive Weapon 58: Tuangou / Swarming Ambush / Flash Mobs

This is a natural Weapon for guerrillas. Big dogs almost never do this. Here's what it's all about:

Think of a swarm of bees or locusts. Or a pack of hungry wolves. You get out of their way—fast! In China, the word *tuangou* means team purchase. There, social media and the internet brings together many like-minded consumers. They show up at a designated day and time at a designated retail store. Acting as a unified group, they demand big discounts on big-ticket items. They've been very successful there. Two similar internet sites in the U.S. that have been somewhat successful are www.groupon.com and www.livingsocial.com.

Here are three other examples:

- *Banzai runs*, where a group of 20 to 50 Mexicans rush across the U.S. border. The Border Patrol can't catch all of them.
- *Speedboats vs. warships*. In war games held in the Persian Gulf, about 30 fast, small (and cheap) speedboats sank 16 major (expensive) warships of the U.S. Navy in ten minutes. Their sheer numbers involved overloaded the warships' ability to handle the attack. *Source*: Don's good buddy, Naval Officer Al Barrera, who was there.
- *Flash robs*. We didn't misspell this. Robs, not mobs. In 2011, the National Retail Association began using this term to describe planned robberies. Stores—big-box and convenience alike—can't handle hordes of people who overload the system by rushing in, grabbing merchandise, and fleeing quickly. Twitter, Facebook, and text messages summon groups to a given store where the mass robberies take place. The NRF has issued guidelines to minimize theft, including police monitoring of social media sites, placing more valuable merchandise at the back of stores, putting clothes on hangers instead of folding them, and good visibility to the outside so employees can call 911 quickly if they see a mob starting to form.

Two Winning Big Dog Counter-Punches

Since big dogs are on the receiving end of this Weapon, here's what they might do when you try it on them:

- They will gather intelligence (Defensive 22, *Get and verify information*) to find out if you and others are planning on doing this to them. Since violence often occurs whenever this Weapon is used, big dogs should probably *Get lost for a while* (Defensive 27). This isn't simply stalling for time. It's a matter of survival, of avoiding a shouting match. That's good for both of you.
- Big dogs might try requesting a postponement (Defensive 27, *Stall for time*), but if they're smart, they know this probably won't work. A smarter big dog will simply tell you he's not going to deal with you anymore (Assertive 73, *Tell TOS you're getting ready to withdraw*).

Assertive Weapon 64: *Take* It First, Then *Talk* About It

Guerrillas who make a habit of winning like to surprise the big dog by taking action first. The idea is to take possession first, then talk about it without offering an apology. Yes, it's a fait accompli. But it's not necessarily a done deal because the big dog may not let your action stand. *On the other hand, it's a lot easier to get the big dog to forgive you than to get his permission in the first place.* So don't be timid.

Three Winning Guerrilla Counter-Punches

When you're dealing with other guerrillas—or even big dogs—who you think might do this, here's what you should do:

- Learn the track record of the people you're dealing with (Assertive 32, *Know your enemy and know yourself—knowledge is power*).
- If you don't know ahead of time what they're capable of, then try *putting on a good show by acting wild and crazy* when they try this on you (Assertive 18).
- Finally, if you have enough money and time and feel it's worthwhile, sue them (Assertive 84, *Intimidate TOS by your money*). But don't waste your time on a *frivolous lawsuit* (Dirty Trick 19).

Assertive Weapon 93: Intimidate the Person You're Dealing with by Being Untouchable

Everybody has been intimidated, especially by big dogs. But some big dogs are more intimidating than others. Don's seminar participants overwhelmingly picked ten kinds of people as the most difficult to deal with. If you want to make a trouble-free and quick deal, we suggest you stay away from:

- Old people—too set in their ways.
- Owners of smaller companies—too dictatorial.
- People who've been with their company for a very long time—too complacent, too inflexible.
- People with prestigious occupations—too big-headed.
- Celebrities—ditto.
- Politicians—too prone to lie.
- Whoever's sleeping with the box—they're *extremely untouchable* (Assertive 93).
- Very good-looking people—too selfish. Why? They've been the center of attention all their lives and use this to get what they want from other people.
- Rude and mean people—too obnoxious. But they're richer, too, and this often makes them attractive targets.
- And if you sell cars or real estate, stay away from police officers. Several of Don's friends own car dealerships. Others are realtors. They told him that cops often blackmailed their salespeople. How? By threatening to arrest them for attempting to defraud them. They dropped the threat only if the salesmen gave them a better deal.

Don's seminar participants also thought certain nationalities and ethnic groups were very difficult to deal with. You can get information about this by going to **www.GuerrillaDon.com**.

Why do these kinds of people cause you more trouble than other potential clients? Because many of them have been the center of attention for a long time. Eventually, they seem to think they can do anything they want, without incurring penalties for their misdeeds. In 2010, Barney Frank, congressman from Massachusetts from 1981 to 2013, said "We're professional people who are used to affection. Voter discontent is almost disorienting." Their egos are huge.

Bottom line: Because they've been untouchable for so long, these kinds of people think they have *Charismatic power* (Assertive 87), but many of them seem to have had *charismatic bypass* operations instead. That's why they use this intimidation Weapon so often. We feel these ten kinds of people are nothing but trouble. Why ask for trouble? Instead, make deals with people who don't fit into any of these categories.

Four Winning Guerrilla Counter-Punches

- Anybody who uses this on you usually isn't worth dealing with in the first place. Don't waste your time—walk away from the deal (Assertive 68, *Elvis has left the building*).
- On the other hand, if you've made the big dog already *invest a lot of his time* in the deal, you've got a lot of leverage over him (Assertive 27).
- Even untouchables know the value of time, too. If you really have to deal with people like this, massage their ego—*Use smooth talk, flattery, and charm* (Assertive 60). This will keep their mind off how much time they're investing in the deal.
- Untouchables are especially susceptible to people who *ooze warmth* (Cooperative 24).

Assertive Weapon 100: Ignore the Big Dog—Have a *Deaf Ear*

Ignore what the big dog tells you and keep on doing things *your* way, not *his* way. Big dogs all over the world tend to use this Weapon fairly often. But it's extremely common in the Middle East, where many big dog decision-makers have a lot of money and power. Expect to be ignored often when you're trying to make deals in that part of the world. Don't let the high level of Arab hospitality fool you. It's superficial. When they deal with Europeans and Americans, Arabs flatter their visitors' egos by pretending to be interested (Dirty Trick 55. *Obvious lying*). Most of the time, they're not, since they already have just about everything they want. After all, they're already rich and powerful. And they get their kicks by seeing their hungry visitors squirm. Don's experience in the Middle East, where he taught marketing at universities in three nations, and did consulting for several years, makes him feel this is one of the top ten negotiating techniques used by Arabs.

For more information about Arab negotiating techniques, please go to **www.GuerrillaDon.com**.

Don and Jay have noticed most American guerrillas seem to be afraid to use this Weapon on the big dog. They shouldn't, because it seems to work very often. Why? Simply because it's so unexpected. And when it *does* work, it works very, very well. Many big dogs will be so shocked when a guerrilla uses it, they won't know what to do. They'll often overlook your insolent behavior, especially on matters they think aren't very important. So ignore what big dogs tell you and keep on doing things *your* way, not *their* way. You'll probably win more often than you think you will.

Two Winning Guerrilla Counter-Punches

- Pretend to be offended when you're ignored (Dirty Trick 55, *Obvious lying*). This may get the big dog's attention.
- And never forget that *Chinese favorite, the rule of three* (Assertive 25). Give up after he ignores your third overture—the prize probably isn't worth wasting your valuable time and effort.

CHAPTER 7

12 DEFENSIVE WEAPONS— POWERFUL AND *UNDER*-USED

What this chapter is all about: *Distraction, commitment and power, silence, body language (four Weapons), concessions, grapevine, excuses, change the subject, and allies.*

Although we both prefer using Assertive Weapons, you can win with Defensive Weapons—and you can win often and win big if you do everything right. Here are three sayings you probably have heard:

- The only real defense is an active defense (Mao Tse-Tung).
- The best offense is a good defense (various sports—also Jay's Golden Rule 40 in Chapter 18).
- Retreating is just advancing in another direction (U.S. Army Field Manual).

Here are the 12 Defensive Weapons that most people don't use very much. Big dogs probably will be surprised when you use them, and this will give you a big advantage.

Defensive Weapon 5: Distract the Big Dog When He's Overly Aggressive, Put Him Off-Balance—Japanese-Style

If *putting the big dog off-balance* sounds familiar, it should. See Assertive Weapon 1—*Make Sudden Unexpected Moves*. But why *Japanese-style*? Because Don learned this long ago when he read Miyamoto Musashi's book, *Go Rin No Sho—The Book of Five Rings—Fire, Air, Earth, Water, and Spirit*. Distracting the big dog puts him off balance, disrupts his rhythm. "Take advantage of his rhythm when he's unsettled, and you'll win," according to Musashi.

The main reason guerrillas use this tactic is to distract the big dog from the issues. Why distract him? Usually, it's because you're weak in some area and don't want to call the big dog's attention to your weakness. Here are six ways you can do this:

- *Dress extra well* (Assertive 42), or *dress very sloppy* (Assertive 43). Calling attention to your physical appearance often distracts the big dog from what you are saying.
- Bring along a very attractive assistant with you (Dirty Trick 48, *Unusually pleasant interruptions*).
- Bring up an issue that has nothing to do with what you and the big dog are discussing (Assertive 5, *Surprise TOS with new issues and broader problems*). Remember, TOS stands for the other side.
- Get out of a traffic ticket by pretending you can't speak. Write each answer in longhand on a yellow pad.
- When Don lived in traffic-clogged Kuala Lumpur, Malaysia, he always carried his doctor's business card in his wallet. Police officers on the other side of the curve in the road often stopped him for driving on the shoulder. Before they said anything to him, he pre-empted them by showing them the business card, quickly said "Jantung, boom-boom, ospital, emergensi, bye-bye" and drove away immediately. (Jantung means *heart* in Bahasa Malaysia.) He claims this distraction technique *never* failed, and he's very proud of thinking of it!
- Another one that works very well for Don is this: Before the cop says anything, he pulls out a map of the city and says, "I'm new in town. I've got to be at the mayor's office in 20 minutes. Very important meeting. I can't figure out this map. Please tell me how to get there."

www.GuerrillaDon.com has 36 other excuses. Some are unique. Some have been heard by cops, over and over. But they all work!

Four Winning Guerrilla Counter-Punches

Let's say another guerrilla or a big dog distracts you. Here are four things you can do:

- As soon as you start feeling distracted and disoriented, try to delay things. For example, be honest and tell him, "I'm not sure. Let me think about it." Two Weapons here: Defensive 27 (*Stall for time*) and Cooperative 10 (*Admit it when you don't know something—don't hide it*).
- Or try this: "Let me check things with my boss. After that, I'll get back to you." This is Dirty Trick 5 (*Limited authority—But first, I have to ask my mommy*).
- Or simply confront him and say "Let's get back to what we were *really* talking about." This is Assertive 52 (*Confront TOS with "Why are you using Dirty Tricks, and when will you stop?"*)
- Never let him get you drunk or high (Dirty Trick 80, *Dull TOS's senses and judgment—deliberately use drugs or alcohol on him*). That's a very powerful distraction Weapon. So be very watchful here.

Defensive Weapon 9: The Person with the *Least* Commitment to the Relationship Has the *Most* Power

Never forget this Weapon. Use it often. Try to appear apathetic, indifferent, and uncaring. Try to make the big dog *think* he needs you more than you need him. If you really need him more than he needs you, then you've got to be a good actor in order to fool him. If the deal is important to him and he thinks you don't care what happens because you have a lot of other options, you've got most of the power and you're going to be a big winner. You might even decide to test him by walking away (Assertive 68, Say *"Take it or leave it"—Elvis has left the building*).

Warning: Big dogs are usually less committed to the relationship than guerrillas. So guerrillas have to be very, very good actors to use this Weapon successfully. Are you a good actor?

Three Winning Guerrilla Counter-Punches

- Whether you're dealing with big dog or other guerrillas, remember this: When they walk away, never go after them. We mean *never!* You lose all power and credibility that way. Instead, remind them you have many other options yourself (Defensive 4, *Remind TOS of their competition—real or imaginary*).

- *Confront* them (Assertive 52) by saying, "If you don't care about my business or me, then why are you even taking the time to talk to me about making a deal?"

- Don't throw good money after bad. Cut your losses. It's easy to do this, since about all you're going to lose is a lot of your valuable time. Tell them, "I don't want to waste my time anymore. You're obviously not that interested." Then leave. Two Weapons here: Assertive 68 (*Take it or leave it—Elvis has left the building*) and Submissive 16 (*Accept defeat and take what you can get—leave well enough alone*).

Defensive Weapon 10: Complete, Total Silence

As we said in Chapter Two, one of the 18 reasons Americans tend to be poor deal-makers is because they're uncomfortable with silence. Guerrillas and big dogs alike. People living in Asian nations, on the other hand, are not only comfortable with silence, they use it as a bargaining Weapon. Don has heard this from many Japanese and Chinese executives: "We love to deal with you Americans. All we have to do is keep our mouths shut. Americans always seem to start talking when we shut up, so we listen, and we listen well. We get a lot of valuable information that way."

Let's take this one step farther: When you talk, you're making a concession without getting anything in return. Why? Because giving away information *is* a concession. A big one. Never make a concession without getting something in return. So train yourself to be quiet—don't give away information needlessly. Two weapons here: Defensive 42 (*Don't give TOS very important information*) and Assertive 32 (*Knowledge is power—whoever has the most knowledge has the most power*).

Finally, here's another hint for you to use when you negotiate with teams of Chinese, Japanese, or Koreans: The person with the most power in the group—the decision-maker—is the person who says the *least*. He lets his subordinates do all the talking. Watch *his* body language carefully (Defensive 15).

Four Winning Guerrilla Counter-Punches

- When the big dog tries this silence technique on you, stare back at him impassively and don't say anything (Defensive 10, *Complete, total silence.* Defensive 11, *Don't react at all, either positively or negatively*). See who breaks down first. But be careful you don't fall asleep while staring.
- Try to break this passive pissing contest by asking some open-ended questions. The big dog can't simply say yes or no—he'll have to start talking. That might break the impasse (Defensive 41, *Keep asking for more and more information*).
- Keep the conversation going by using *Active listening* (Cooperative 15). We'll tell you how to do this in Chapter 8.

Defensive Weapon 15: Watch the Other Guy's Body Language Very Closely

This is such an important Weapon that Chapter 16, Guerrilla Body Language, is devoted to it. We think it's going to be your favorite chapter. Read it very carefully. You'll learn what each gesture means. Then, carefully watch the body language of the person you're dealing with, and you'll soon know what's on his mind. But don't let him know you're watching him for clues. And never, ever take notes. Simply watch him for about five minutes. Put each gesture into either a positive or negative category. If the big dog or another guerrilla is making mostly positive gestures, keep doing whatever you're doing, because it's working for you. If he's making mostly negative gestures, stop doing whatever you're doing and try something different, because it's not working.

One Winning Guerrilla Counter-Punch

Right now, all we'll tell you is this: Use positive gestures if you want to make the big dog or another guerrilla think you like what he's telling you. Use negative gestures if you want him to think you're rejecting what he says. By doing this, you're really *Manipulating him with your own body language*. This is Defensive Weapon 16—coming right up!

Defensive Weapon 16: Manipulate the Other Guy With Your Own Body Language

This is easy to do. Or *is* it? If the big dog or another guerrilla is making negative gestures toward you, don't be tempted to mirror or mimic him by making negative gestures. If you make negative gestures in return, the deal-making process will be on a downward spiral that will be hard to reverse. Instead, avoid the temptation to be negative in return. Make positive gestures instead. He will find it hard not to do the same. And you'll automatically begin thinking positively, too. Your negotiation will begin an upward spiral.

Why does this underused technique work so well? Here are two big reasons:

- Likes attract. Opposites don't attract.
- A scholarly study found that a deal was reached 67 percent of the time when negotiator A was instructed to mirror negotiator B's body language. A deal was reached only 12 percent of the time when negotiator A was instructed *not* to mirror negotiator B's body language.

Two Winning Guerrilla Counter-Punches

- Learn as much as you can about body language (Defensive Weapons 15-19). Then you'll know when anybody—friends, relatives, strangers, big dogs and guerrillas alike—are using their body language to manipulate you. And you'll know how to use your own body language to influence them—either positively or negatively.
- Design your sales pitches and proposals so that the big dog thinks to himself, "Wow, both of us have a lot in common." Why? Google the *Framingham Heart Study* and *social contagion* and find out now. Or wait till you read about this in Chapter 16, page 200.

Defensive Weapon 18: Use Touch Power—the Body Language of Touching

How do big dogs and guerrillas react when you touch them? Most of the time, touching people establishes rapport with them, so we recommend you do it. It's usually not expected, and most people interpret it as friendly. But be cautious. Don't over-do it. It may backfire, especially when you are dealing with somebody of the opposite sex. Here are three other things to think about:

- Never poke other people—that's a hostile gesture. Neither big dogs nor guerrillas like it.
- You're always invading other people's space when you touch them. That can be dangerous. Think how you would feel you're on the receiving end of the touch.
- But if you and the other person are friends and approximately the same age, touching is probably OK.

Two Winning Guerrilla Counter-Punches

- If the big dog touches you a lot without poking you, he's probably going to be receptive to your deal. If he doesn't, then *use positive body language* to get him in a better mood (Defensive 16).
- And after he's in a better mood, reinforce that mood by occasionally touching him back (Defensive 18, *Touch power*).

Defensive Weapon 19: Use Position Power— the Language Spoken by Office Furniture

There are many power points in an office. If the big dog occupies them and keeps you from occupying them, he's trying to dominate you. Once again, Chapter 16 discusses them in detail. Check out the 4 drawings on pages 197-199 now if you want.

One Winning Guerrilla Counter-Punch

If you and several others are going to meet in somebody else's office, get there early (Preparation 2, *Prepare, rehearse, manage your time*). Occupy power positions in the room before somebody else does. On the other hand, if you don't want to be noticed, then pick the least powerful position in the room. And if you're one-on-one with the big dog, don't let him maneuver you into a weak position.

Defensive Weapon 20: Carefully Observe the Concession Patterns of Both You and the Big Dog—and Keep a Record of Them

Like body language, making concessions is such an important Weapon that Chapter 17, Guerrilla Concession-Making, is devoted to it. There's lots of valuable stuff to learn there. Right now, though, here are the essentials you need to know:

- Write down precisely *what* both you and the big dog concede.
- Also write down *when* you and he make concessions.
- It may or may not be wise to let the big dog seeing you take notes. Do what doesn't irritate him or make him suspicious. You've got to know him pretty well, though. If you don't, you'll guess wrong.
- Look for patterns, especially the seven you see in Chapter 17. Learning the patterns of the big dog's concession patterns gives you a lot of power, but it isn't used very often.

Four Winning Guerrilla Counter-Punches

Here's what to do when you think the big dog or another guerrilla is recording and analyzing your concession patterns:

- Try to be ambiguous and unpredictable, so the big dog will be too unsettled to figure out your overall concession pattern. Two Weapons: Assertive 1 (*Make sudden, unexpected moves*) and Defensive 53 (*Use Creative Vagueness*).
- Make sure he thinks your concessions hurt you, so show pain if you think that will work. Two weapons once again: Assertive 16 (*Show pain when you concede*) and Dirty Trick 55 (*Obvious lying, not exaggerated big talk*). Don't give anything away too easily.
- Watch the big dog. Record what he does. If he gives you a concession too quickly, it probably doesn't mean much to him. This means you'll probably be able to get a lot more from him (Defensive 20, *Carefully observe TOS's concession patterns*).
- *Watch his body language closely* to see if his concessions mean a lot or just a little to him (Defensive 15). Arm yourself with this information and, once again, you'll be able to get a lot more from him. Treat this information like a very powerful Weapon, because that's exactly what it is.

Defensive Weapon 24: Grapevine Gossip

It's very easy to manipulate both big dogs and guerrillas using the grapevine. People seem to believe grapevine gossip more than they believe their own eyes. A study by the National Academy of Sciences said that positive grapevine gossip *increased* other people's cooperation level by 20 percent. Negative grapevine gossip *decreased* the level by 20 percent. This happens even when they already have all the information. Why? Because gossip from other people makes them think that somehow they've missed something important.

What's the obvious problem here? Making sure that the information you give to the grapevine is the same information they get. It often gets distorted in the process of one person telling the next person. And you have no control over the process itself.

Four Winning Guerrilla Counter-Punches

- Don't believe all you hear about big dogs or other guerrillas, especially if what's being said comes from the grapevine—the rumor may be planted by the big dog or the guerrilla himself. And rumors are often wrong (Preparation 7, *Become hard to convince*). Please go to **www.GuerrillaDon.com**,where you'll learn the following things about rumors—why people spread them, under what conditions rumors work and don't work, what you can do about rumors concerning you, what you should *never* do about those rumors, and the kinds of rumors that spread the fastest. Armed with this knowledge, you can be a very effective rumor-spreader. And rumor-stopper.
- Talk directly with the people who are leaking the information to you and make an eyeball-to-eyeball assessment of them. Pay special attention to their *body language* (Defensive 15). They may be working for the big dog.
- Be very critical of the sources of information. Make sure they're reliable, and make sure you're able to check the validity of the information (Defensive 22, *Get and verify information*).
- Monitor your employees so they don't leak information on the grapevine to the other side (Use Assertive 55, *Limit what your team can tell TOS*).

Defensive Weapon 47: My Dog Ate My Homework

Yes, this is under-used. Most people know about it and think it's too obvious, and that's why they don't use it very often. The unexpectedness of it is what makes it so powerful. You already know how it works: If you want to delay things, take a tip from students all over the world who didn't bring their homework to school. Tell the big dog or the other guerrilla you've lost a large amount of data because your computer crashed. Say, "This information is crucial to our negotiation, and I have to reconstruct it from memory."

Four Winning Guerrilla Counter-Punches
- *Watch the body language* of the person using this lame excuse—the big dog or another guerrilla. Why? To see if he's lying (Defensive 15).
- If he's obviously lying, break off negotiations then and there (Assertive 68, *Walk away—Elvis has left the building*).
- Or set a *deadline* (Assertive 28).
- In the meantime, look for somebody else to make a deal with, and tell the other guy you're doing this (Defensive 4. *Remind TOS of his competition—real or imaginary*).

Defensive Weapon 58: Get Off the Subject for a While— Lighten Up by Using Humor, Talking About Sports, Etc.

This doesn't sound powerful, but it really is. It's a good way of stalling for time and defusing a volatile situation. And it works well on both big dogs and other guerrillas. Here are five other benefits:

- It reduces hostility and tension.
- It makes the big dog listen more.
- It improves morale and rapport.
- It often improves trust.
- Here's the most important benefit: Because the big dog or the other guerrilla now thinks you're his friend, he may give you a better deal— more concessions, in other words.

Don't bring up religion or politics, though. No matter what you say, you'll probably offend somebody. And, in our opinion, talking about sex has more negatives than positives.

Three Winning Guerrilla Counter-Punches

- Have a reservoir of jokes handy so you can pull them out as needed (Preparation 2, *Prepare, rehearse, manage your time*). Don has had great results using jokes from Rodney Dangerfield and George Carlin in his seminars and when he is negotiating deals. You'll find a lot of them on the internet.
- But don't try to come up with a better joke or a better sports story than the big dog told you. This isn't a pissing contest (Submissive 16, *Leave well enough alone*).
- Have you documented the reactions to your jokes? Try it. You might be surprised to learn which ones work and which ones don't (Assertive 32, *Knowledge is power*).

Defensive Weapon 76: Find Allies and Use Them

Look for others who are willing to help you. Ask them to act on your behalf, either directly or indirectly. They can be inside or outside of the big dog's company. They can also be inside or outside of *your* company. And we suggest you even go one major step farther—bond with the big dog, too. Make him your ally (Cooperative 5, *Get the best ally of all—TOS himself*). Here's a quick way for you to do this: Don't just tell the big dog about your satisfied customers—arrange for him to meet with them.

Three Winning Guerrilla Counter-Punches

- If you think the big dog or another guerrilla is trying to get people in your company to say good things about him, do this: Try and find out how much he knows about your organization and whom he knows (Assertive 32, *Knowledge is power*). Talk to the people he knows, and find out what's going on.
- Don't let him develop allies in your organization (Defensive 76, *Find allies and use them*). This isn't being a control freak—it's simply making sure he doesn't get important information about you which you don't want him to know.
- Finally, put strict *limits on what members of your team can tell the big dog or other guerrilla* outside of the bargaining situation (Assertive 55). This may be hard to enforce, though.

CHAPTER 8

EIGHT COOPERATIVE WEAPONS– POWERFUL AND *UNDER*-USED

 hat this chapter is all about: Patience, admit you don't know, listening (two Weapons), leave something extra (a bonus) on the table, make him look good, make him think you lost, and become indispensable.

Cooperative Weapon 1: Power of Patience

There are no powerful *Submissive* Weapons that are under-used, and that's why we don't have a chapter on this subject. Instead, Chapter Eight is about the eight powerful under-used *Cooperative* Weapons.

If you can afford to outwait the person you're trying to make a deal with, you'll probably win big—especially if he can't afford to outwait you (Assertive 27, *Make the other person invest a lot of his time*). This applies to big dogs and other guerrillas alike. This is why so many foreigners love to negotiate with impatient Americans—they know if they stall long enough, the Americans will capitulate and give in to almost anything. You'll remember we talked about this in Chapter Two—the eighth reason Americans are poor negotiators. Here are five of the many benefits of being more patient than the big dog:

- He'll probably give you more concessions.
- You'll have more time to evaluate pro's and con's of his offer.
- This moves him away from his *wish list* to his *reality list* (Assertive 56).
- You'll get a lot more new information from him.
- You'll feel more in control, less stressful, less overwhelmed by events.

Four Winning Guerrilla Counter-Punches

- Why talk about counter-punches when the big dog or the other guerrilla is already cooperating with you, giving you what you want? Most of the time you should simply accept what he's doing (Submissive 16, *Take what you can get—leave well enough alone*).
- However—and there always seems to be a however—if he seems *overly* patient with you, make sure he's not just taking an extended time out (Defensive 22, *Get and verify information—detect and expose bullshit*).
- And eventually, you'll have to negotiate reasonable *deadlines* with him (Assertive 28).
- Finally, don't forget to take advantage of the big dog's patience by reviewing your position and getting rid of obstacles. You'll be stronger the next time you meet again (Preparation 1, *Think ahead— circumstances are always changing*).

Cooperative Weapon 10: Admit You Don't Know Something—Don't Hide It

This Weapon is powerful because it's so unexpected. Simply tell the big dog you don't have sufficient information—then tell him you'll get it. And then, make sure you tell him *when* you'll get it. Make sure you don't miss your self-imposed deadline (Assertive 28, *Use deadlines wisely*). Here's a big plus: He'll probably admire you for your honesty. He may even help you get the information, because he's become your ally (Cooperative 5, *Get the best ally of all—TOS himself*). Caution: This works better on big dogs than on other guerrillas. And, once again, please remember TOS stands for the other side.

Three Winning Guerrilla Counter-Punches

- When the big dog tells you he doesn't know something, be skeptical at first (Preparation 7, *Become hard to convince*).

- Watch his *body language* to see if he's lying (Defensive 15). He may just be trying to delay things or to get your guard down.
- And be sure to thank him in a warm manner for being honest with you (Assertive 60, *Use smooth talk, flattery, and charm*).

Cooperative Weapon 14: The Cheapest Concession of All—Listen, and Listen Well

How arrogant are you? Don't be so arrogant that you do all the talking. *Listening is the cheapest—and most important—concession you can make.* It pays big dividends, because more *knowledge makes you more powerful* (Assertive 32). Listen for important details. They won't come too easily—until the person you're dealing with starts trusting you. Remember, *you have to earn the right to learn the other person's needs* (Preparation 5). And don't forget that you *flatter* both big dogs and other guerrillas when you listen to them. You *insult* them when you don't.

> Some venues are listener-friendly, some aren't. The worst place Don remembers is the Pan-Afrique, a five-star hotel in Nairobi. Kenya. His seminar there was held in the hotel's night club. It overlooked the swimming pool. The pool was closed that day. Why? Because a TV crew was filming a commercial that morning, using eight extremely beautiful women in bikinis. Thirty-eight of the 40 people at the seminar were men. Don got a lot of boo's when he reluctantly asked the concierge to put up white sheets over the plate glass windows. He made sure all of his future seminars were held in function rooms with no distractions.

Two Winning Guerrilla Counter-Punches

- Be very cautious when you're dealing with big dogs and other guerrillas who are good listeners (Preparation 7, *Become hard to convince*). You may end up telling them a lot more than you ever intended.
- On the other hand, when you deal with a good listener, you have a great opportunity to share the kind of information that puts your needs and interests in the best light (Cooperative 20, *Mental seduction*).

Cooperative Weapon 15: Master
Active Listening and Use It Often

If your deal-making procedure is stalled, try using the other person's own words to emphasize the points you agree upon. This works on both big dogs and other guerrillas.

Here's how you can use this Weapon to get more from anybody you're dealing with. Only eight things to remember:

- Watch his body language while he's speaking. It will tell you if he's sincere or trying to hide something.
- Focus on him. Listen intently, but not just to his words. Listen to his tone of voice.
- Listen for the feeling underneath those words—that's *even more* important.
- When he pauses, start paraphrasing his words. This doesn't mean agreeing with him. And this doesn't mean repeating his words verbatim. Doing this will make him think you're mocking him. Say something like this: "You seem to feel upset. Is this because…?"
- If what he says isn't that clear to you, ask him questions. But don't interrupt him.
- Make sure your own feelings don't influence the way you listen to him.
- Don't be uncomfortable with silent periods. Expect them. Ask lots of open-ended questions.
- Finally, don't think about what you're going to say when he stops talking. Say focused on him.

Are you skeptical about this? Here's a recent study published in a scholarly journal: Who gets bigger tips at a restaurant? Waiter A, who takes your order, tells you OK, then goes away. Or Waiter B, who takes your order and repeats *almost exactly* what each person wants, then goes away? Answer: Waiter B got 70 percent higher tips. Active listening works, big-time!

Five Winning Guerrilla Counter-Punches
- When big dogs or other guerrillas use this Weapon on you, welcome it. Don't fight it (Submission 16, *Leave well enough alone*). It indicates

the other person cares enough and is interested enough in what you're telling him, and that he is using it to find out more about you and what you're offering him.

- But be cautious, perhaps even afraid, if you have something to hide. His use of active listening may help him learn the truth. Don't let your fear show (Assertive 70, *Be brave, not scared*).
- You might want to take a break to compose yourself (Defensive 27, *Stall for time—get lost for a while*). Maybe *go to the toilet*, even if you don't have the urge (Defensive 50).
- So listen carefully to what the big dog says in response to what you tell him (Cooperative 14, *Listen, and listen well*). It's pretty easy to tell if he's using active listening on you.

If you don't know that much about this powerful technique, go to **www.GuerrillaDon.com**. You'll learn more there.

Cooperative Weapon 16: The Bonus—Leave Something Extra on the Table at the End

This doesn't mean you should make an extra concession *before* the deal has been completed. This is about giving something nice and unexpected to the big dog or the other guerrilla *after* the deal has been completed and the contract has been signed. The bonus is a nice and simple way of telling him "Thank you." Here are two examples, one good, one bad:

- Good: A very successful dentist gives his patient a coupon for dinner for two at an expensive restaurant after his patient has received implants.
- Bad: Presenters at the Academy Awards who receive no fees, get a *goodie-bag* of jewelry and other expensive merchandise at the end of the ceremony. The first year this was done it was unexpected, and presenters were grateful. Today, it's expected, and presenters often bad-mouth the Academy for not giving them more stuff to take home. Celebrities' sense of entitlement is always high, but it's even higher at the Academy Awards. (We'll talk more about this in Chapter 14 when we discuss Cooperative Weapon 4.)

Be very careful when you use this Weapon, because you may get results you don't expect. Here's what we mean:

- The value of any item declines in the other guy's mind when you offer it to him as a gift.
- Don't make the extra bonus too big. Why not? Because your customers may think something's wrong with your gift—it might be out of style or obsolete.
- Sometimes, you should avoid using the word *free*. Many people see only zero's in their mind when they hear that word. It might be better to say instead, "Here's a $100 coupon to use at your next visit to this five-star hotel." People will see $100 instead of zero's.

Three Winning Guerrilla Counter-Punches
- Accept the gift with gratitude—don't ask him "Why are you giving me this?" This is Submissive Weapon 16, *Leave well enough alone*).
- But also be cautious. Ask your attorney if the goodies are bribes. If they are and if you can get in trouble keeping them, return them (Defensive 33, *I won't break the law*).
- But appear grateful, even after you return the goodies. Return them in a gracious and thankful manner (Cooperative 24, *Ooze warmth*).

Cooperative Weapon 18: Make Sure the Other Person Looks Good at the End

If the person you're trying to make a deal with doesn't own the company, show him how coming to an agreement with you, buying your product or service, will help him in the eyes of his boss. He'll appreciate it, and you'll start developing rapport with him. Eventually, you'll be able to help him overcome his weakness and optimize the positive things he already has going for him.

Two Winning Guerrilla Counter-Punches
- If the big dog tries to make you look good, he's probably sincere. If so, accept his offer, but not too quickly (Assertive 24, *Avoid buyer's remorse—don't accept TOS's offer too quickly*).
- And always *watch his body language* to see if he's sincere or not (Defensive 15).

Cooperative Weapon 19: Make the Big Dog Think You Lost, Even if You Won Big…Think of the Movie, *The Sting*

At the end of a well-known movie from the 1970s, *The Sting*, the bad guys were going to kill the heroes and take their money. Before that happened, though, federal agents burst through the door and killed the heroes. The bad guys left in a hurry before the feds saw them—and they had to leave the money behind. It turned out the heroes faked their deaths and were partners with the phony federal agents. They split the money, and the bad guys didn't try to go after them, because they thought they were dead.

Here's the moral of the story: *Lose your ego* (Preparation 10). Even if you won, don't gloat about it. If the big dog thinks you won too much, he may try to back out of the deal. Or worse, he may try to take revenge on you (Dirty Trick 6, *Revenge—ruin TOS's victory celebration*). To learn more about how to deal with revenge-takers, go to **www.GuerrillaDon.com**.

Three Winning Guerrilla Counter-Punches

- Watch out if big dogs or other guerrillas tell you they're going to lose too much money by making the deal with you—and then sign the deal after all (Preparation 7, *Become hard to convince*). They're probably lying—they made a lot of money.
- So don't be an eager beaver—*don't accept their offer too quickly* (Assertive 24). You'll probably get more if you wait (Cooperative 1, *Power of patience*).
- And if you think he's backed himself into a corner, help him out without making him lose face (Cooperative 17, *When you win big, make sure TOS saves face*).

Cooperative Weapon 20: Mental Seduction—Become Indispensable to the Big Dog by *Over*-Cooperating with Him

Try to get the big dog to depend on you. Make him trust you by going far, far beyond the call of duty. There's a big negative side to this, though: If you take this too far and are *very* successful at doing this, you'll isolate him, and this may create a *siege mentality*, the illusion that his enemies are lurking everywhere. So don't go *too far* beyond the call of duty.

Three Winning Guerrilla Counter-Punches

It's hard to stop depending on the big dog if you've allowed him to get this far with you. Here's how to get out of your dependence:

- Watch out if he tries to *go above and beyond the call of duty* (Cooperative Weapons 21 and 22) too often. Try to figure out why this is happening (Preparation 7, *Become hard to convince*).
- Also watch out if the big dog is your boss and tries to isolate you by censoring your phone calls and turning away visitors. He's using a variation of Dirty Trick 29 on you (*Isolate TOS*). If you have strong, trusted *gatekeepers* (Assertive 34) who have your best interest at heart, this probably won't happen. So use them.
- This won't happen either if you're a skeptic at heart (Preparation 7, Become hard to convince) and not gullible (Dirty Trick 76, *The Two G-spots: Greed and gullibility*).

CHAPTER 9

EIGHT DIRTY TRICKS— POWERFUL AND *UNDER*-USED

What this chapter is all about: Backing the big dog into a corner, two contract tricks, bait-and-switch, becoming untouchable, pretending you know, frightening ambiance and music, and embarrassing him.

Dirty Tricks are a part of everyday life. We don't recommend their use, not by you, not by anyone. They're counterproductive. They're not fair. Sometimes, they're even illegal. The person you're trying to make a deal with, whether he's a big dog or another guerrilla, doesn't like them. Once he knows you're using them, he'll almost certainly try to get even with you as soon as possible. This book of yours is about *serious* deal-making with *serious* people. It's not about scams pulled by con artists. Go to **www.GuerrillaDon.com** for details of 76 scams and cons. Only 14 of them are in here in your book—Dirty Tricks 62-75. See Chapter Four.

We talk about Dirty Tricks simply because they're used so much—especially by guerrillas. You need to recognize them as soon as possible and to have a large reservoir of counter-punches ready to use when they're used against you.

To tell if somebody is using Dirty Tricks or not, look once again at Cooperative Weapon 20, which we just finished discussing—*Mental Seduction*.

It's about creating trust by going far, far beyond the call of duty. If your motive in becoming indispensable by over-cooperating is to help both of you make more profits, it's a Cooperative Weapon. If your motive is to isolate the other guy from his friends and relatives and take over his affairs just to advance yourself, that's more than just manipulation—that's a Dirty Trick.

Is seduction itself a Dirty Trick? We don't think seducing other people is offensive. It's actually a compliment to them. You're flattering them, and you're relieving them of boredom. And if they don't respond positively to your flirtation efforts, it's not because you're doing something wrong—you're just doing it the wrong way. And if you're trying to sell the other person something in your business, you'll be successful a great deal of the time if you do it the *right* way, not the *wrong* way.

So, we're not going to pass judgments on your motives. All we want to do is tell you about Don's 100 most powerful Weapons that will make you much better at getting other people to do what you want them to do. Call your actions whatever you like—seduction, manipulation, persuasion, influence, negotiation, making a deal. Just do it well, and you'll be very pleased with the outcome. And we'll be pleased too, because we'll know that we've helped you accomplish something important.

Now, let's look at the eight most powerful yet under-used Dirty Tricks:

Dirty Trick 1: Make It Impossible for the Big Dog to Go Somewhere Else at the Last Minute

Stall until the deadline set by the big dog or the other guerrilla is almost there—then, demand a lot more money or other goodies from him. Watch out if he tries to get you to rely on him early in the deal-making process. He'll over-cooperate with you at this courtship stage so you'll feel he's indispensable (Cooperative Weapons 5 and 20—*Get the best ally of all—TOS himself* and *Mental seduction*). (Once again, TOS stands for the other side.) All he wants is to make you commit to the deal by making it hard or even impossible for you to go somewhere else to get what you want. Here are two examples of these kinds of con games:

A smooth-talking retailer convinces you to pay a nonrefundable deposit. He phones you and says "It's here." But when you come to the store to pick it up, he says it's not available. He tries to get you to buy a different brand—at a higher price, of course (Dirty Trick 16, *Seller's bait-and-switch*).

Although you don't really want the person you're dealing with to know your deadline, he gets you to trust him so much that you reveal it to him. He then stalls on purpose until just before your deadline (Defensive 27, *Stall for time—get lost for a while*). Then he tells you he'll do the job right away but at a much higher price (Dirty Trick 16 again) .You pay it because you've stopped looking for somebody else, and you're desperate (Assertive 28, *Deadlines*). Think: Plumber stalls and then shows up just before your important party and demands more money.

Two Winning Guerrilla Counter-Punches

- Notice that the first con artist we talked about here used two Cooperative Weapons (5 and 20) to gain your trust. That's typical. Be skeptical when somebody over-cooperates. Don't trust people who seem too good to be true very much. *Become hard to convince* (Preparation 7). Don't trust your friends too much. Or even your spouse. She won't give you her passwords, and you won't give them to her either. Are we correct? We'll talk about passwords again in Chapter 12.

- And, of course, *watch out for scams—never pay in advance* (Assertive 65).

Dirty Trick 3: Sign Contract, Escalate Immediately

After both of you have reached an agreement and you have your pen in hand, ready to sign, stop! Ask the big dog or the other guerrilla for more just before you sign the contract. The *extra* you ask for is minor, not major. Like all Dirty Tricks, this is unethical, but it almost always works. Example: "Oh, by the way, throw in the extended warranty instead of the normal warranty—at no cost to me."

Five Winning Guerrilla Counter-Punches

- Don't use *sarcasm* (Assertive 2) on a guy who pulls this trick on you, especially on older people. For example, never tell an old person, "Sir, at your age, you shouldn't even buy green bananas." Instead, take the high moral ground and say, "We negotiated in good faith and we've already agreed to the terms in our contract. If you weren't happy, you should have told me earlier. I don't have the time or the inclination to re-negotiate with you about this. This has left a bad taste in my mouth." This is Dirty Trick 26 (*Phony sanctimony*)—minus the phony part. Wait and see what happens. If he still persists, you may want to use Assertive 68 and tell him, *"Elvis has left the building."*

- So *don't give in* (Defensive 89). Remember, if you agree to his escalation demands, he'll try it again and again.
- Find out as much as you can about him (Assertive 32, *Know your enemy and know yourself*). Does he escalate a lot? If so, don't agree to a deal close to your bottom line. Make sure the deal you're about to sign will give you a lot of profits.
- Be on the alert—guerrillas do this a lot more than big dogs do (Preparation 7, *Become hard to convince*).
- Finally, to keep this from happening in the first place, make sure you phone your boss in his presence and tell him the deal has been finalized (Dirty Trick 5, *Limited authority—But first, I have to ask my mommy*). After his escalation, tell him you can't accept his escalation because you don't want to get in trouble with your boss. Two Weapons here: Assertive 86, *Legitimate power*. Defensive 31, *Be overly bureaucratic*.

Dirty Trick 4: Sign Contract, Re-Negotiate Immediately

Re-open the bargaining right after you sign the contract. If the big dog tries to do this to you, the signed contract probably is not worth much, for he didn't plan to live up to it in the first place. At least not in most western nations. (See reason 14 why Americans are poor negotiators. It's in Chapter Two.)

However, you need to remember this very important cultural difference which we talked about in Chapter Two: Negotiators in many non-Western nations think of detailed, signed contracts as just the *beginning* of an ongoing negotiation that lasts as long as the business relationship lasts. Negotiators in Western nations perceive a detailed, signed contract as the *end* of a negotiation and expect the other side to live up to the details of the signed contract. For details about the non-Western nations where this often happens, go to **www.GuerrillaDon.com**.

By the way, both big dogs and guerrillas tend to do this. It's not just a Weapon by and for big dogs.

Five Winning Guerrilla Counter-Punches

If you're from a Western nation and are negotiating with, for example, Chinese or Thai executives, be aware of this cultural difference. If both you and the person you're dealing with are both from the U.S., here are five things you can do:

- Turn the deal down and start *walking away* (Assertive 73). See if the big dog or other guerrilla tries to stop you. If he does, he needs the deal more than you do, and you have the most power.
- Tell him, "I already told my boss the deal is signed, and he's going to be extremely angry at me if I tell him about this. I won't do it." This is Dirty Trick 5 (*Limited authority—but first, I have to ask my mommy*).
- Show him how angry you are. Use a *mild* combination of Assertive 101 (*Pretend to lose your temper*) and Dirty Trick 51 (*Scare the hell out of TOS*).
- And don't be afraid to do this (Assertive 70, *Be brave, not scared*).

You might be able to stop this from happening in the first place by requiring a large security deposit from the other side as part of the written contract. Make sure it's paid when the contract is signed. Refuse to give back the deposit if they try to re-negotiate and you don't like what they're now asking (Preparation 1, *Think ahead—circumstances are always changing*).

Dirty Trick 16: Seller's Bait-and-Switch

You've seen this often in retailers' ads. When you try to buy something advertised at a store at a low price, the salesman tells you how bad that product is and tries to get you to buy something else—at a much higher price. Sometimes, he will tell you, "Sorry, we're sold out. Try this substitute instead—it's just as good." Or a car dealer tells you, "The car in the ad is way in the back of our lot. Behind ten rows of other cars. It will take about an hour for us to get it out so you can test-drive it."

But this Dirty Trick isn't very common in high-level deal-making. When it *is* used, here's how it usually goes: A guerrilla attract a potential big dog client by *making very attractive promises* of a non-sexual nature (Cooperative 13). Then when the big dog's anxious to buy, the guerrilla tries to get him to accept something else by saying, "I can't do that anymore."

Three Winning Guerrilla Counter-Punches

- Find out as much as you can about the seller (Defensive 22, *Get and verify information*). Avoid him if he uses bait-and-switch a lot.
- Don't just *threaten to walk out* (Assertive 73). Go ahead and *do* it—walk out (Assertive 68, *Elvis has left the building*).
- We've heard of lawsuits against sellers who try this. This is a variation of Dirty Trick 19 (*Frivolous lawsuit to harass TOS*). We don't recommend it, though. Three reasons:
  - ○ It's hard to get proof.
  - ○ Damages are usually negligible. So it's not cost-effective, just a big waste of time.
  - ○ Most of all, when you try this, the negotiating process is over. Is that really what you want?

Dirty Trick 25: Act Untouchable—Claim "I'm Entitled to Special Privileges"

Many people make this claim and want special favors from you. It's probably happened to you many times in your business career. So let's get right into the winning guerrilla counter-punches:

Four Winning Guerrilla Counter-Punches

- First of all, be careful who you deal with. In Chapter Six, we advised you to stay away from ten kinds of big dogs and big dog wanna-be's: Old people, those with a prestigious occupation, politicians, celebrities, very good-looking people, and somebody who either owns the company or has been with the company for a long time (Assertive 93). They think they're untouchable, and they're too demanding. Cops and people who are rude and mean also give you trouble. There are other kinds of untouchables, including people who are sleeping with the boss, ethnic groups protected by laws in some countries, etc. They tend to ask for too much—and they expect to get it. When you deal with them, be very, very careful. Treating them the wrong way may get you into a lot of trouble.
- Know the law, especially overseas (Assertive 32, *Knowledge is power*). For example, in Malaysia, only companies controlled by Malays are considered for government construction projects, So foreign firms give

50.1 percent of the stock to a Malay with friends in the government. He becomes the titular head of the company and does absolutely nothing in return for a fat paycheck. In Saudi Arabia, women can't own their own businesses. But they get around it by signing a contract with a male who becomes the titular head of the company. The woman runs the company, and the guy does nothing at all, except show up once a month to pick up his payoff.

- If you want the contract bad enough, you should do the same thing—even though the local guy doesn't do a damn thing (Submissive 16, *Accept defeat and take what you can get—leave well enough alone*). Don't do this, though, unless you can make enough money, too.

- Remember that if the big dog or the other guerrilla has already *invested a lot of his time* in the deal, you've got a lot of leverage over him (Assertive 27). If this is the case, ignore his claim to special privileges. Instead, threaten to walk away from the deal (Assertive 68, *Say "Take it or leave it"—Elvis has left the building*).

Dirty Trick 27: Act Smug—Make the Big Dog or the Other Guerrilla Think You Already Know a Lot About Him and His Company

Surprise the big dog or another guerrilla by showing him you've done your homework. That you know a lot about him. Be specific.

This will not only surprise him—it will flatter him. Why? Because he knows you think he's important enough to do research on. On the other hand, it may make him fear you. He'll probably ask himself, "Is he trying to make me afraid of his power, or is he trying to be my friend?"

What you *really* want to do is impress the person you're dealing with by showing him you've done your homework and know what his weaknesses and strengths really are.

And here's an extra benefit—you'll put him off-balance. You'll shock him when he realizes you know so much about him.

Three Winning Guerrilla Counter-Punches

What kind of information does the big dog or other guerrilla have about you?

- Watch out if he knows a lot about you—he might already know your bottom line. So ask him probing questions (Defensive 22, *Get and verify information—detect and expose bullshit*).
- If he's got the wrong information, correct him in a polite manner, especially if it's to your advantage to do so. This is a combination of Assertive 60 (*Smooth talk, flattery, and charm*) and Cooperative 17 (*Make sure TOS saves face*).
- If he confronts you with correct information about yourself and your company, you've got to make a decision: Will you bluff your way through your encounter and try to convince him he's wrong? This is Assertive Weapon 50, *Bluffing—not-too-obvious lying*. Or will you be *completely honest* (Cooperative 8) and tell him he's right? Here's what we suggest: Don't lie to him. Adopt this attitude: If he already knows a lot about you, make him your ally (Cooperative 5, *Get the best ally of all—TOS himself*).

Dirty Trick 38: Frightening Ambience, Manipulative Music

The sum total of your entire deal-making experience in the office of the person you're trying to make a deal with can either be pleasant or unpleasant. If the big dog or the other guerrilla is trying to intimidate you, here are some things he may try:

- Background music too loud and not the kind you like. Let's assume he uses Defensive 22 (*Get and verify information*) and finds out you don't like Barry Manilow music, so he plays it all the time you're visiting him. A mall in Christchurch, New Zealand, played Manilow CDs to get rid of "rowdy" teenagers. Interrogators at Guantanamo Bay Prison used the theme from Sesame Street, while rap singer Eminem's *The Real Slim Shady* was used at a CIA prison in Afghanistan.
- His office is above a slightly vibrating generator.
- Stained ceiling and floor tiles.
- Flickering lighting.
- Plus Dirty Icing on the Dirty Cake—a *filthy visitor's toilet* (Dirty Trick 43).

Three Winning Guerrilla Counter-Punches

- When you first visit his office, sensitize yourself. See if you feel comfortable or uncomfortable, perhaps intimidated. If you feel comfortable, the deal-making process will probably be a good one. If not, it won't—unless you change the venue. Perhaps to your own office (Assertive 10, *Location surprise*).

- If what he's doing bothers you big-time, confront the big dog. This is Assertive 52 (*Ask him "Why are you using Dirty Tricks, and when will you stop*). Tell him you're *getting ready to walk out*—and let him know why (Assertive 73).

- If all else fails, simply walk out (Assertive 68, *Elvis has left the building*).

How sensitive are you to your environment? Let's say you're being interviewed for a job. Ask yourself these questions: How do you react when

- You enter the interviewer's office and there's a leather briefcase with sharp edges on the desk?
- You enter somebody's office, and there's nothing on the desk—not even one piece of paper?
- You sit on a hard chair?
- You sit on a soft, comfortable chair?
- You're offered a cup of hot coffee or tea?
- You're offered a glass of iced tea or cold soft drink?

Here's what an article in a scholarly journal says:

- Sharp edges on leather briefcase: Most people become more aggressive.
- Absolutely nothing on large desk: Most become intimidated.
- Hard chair: Most become harder to influence.
- Easy chair: Most become easier to influence.
- Hot coffee or tea: Most become more generous and caring.
- Iced tea or cold soft drink: Most become less generous and caring.

We agree with the article. Do you?

Dirty Trick 77: Put the Big Dog and the Other Guerrilla on the Defensive—Deliberately Embarrass Him, but Only Slightly

Embarrassing the other person is easy to do in Asian nations, but not in the U.S. Remember what we said in Chapter Two—one of the 18 reasons Americans are sub-par deal-makers overseas is that Americans don't get embarrassed very easy. A high-level Japanese business executive once told Don, "Americans have a very low sense of shame. They don't even know when they're embarrassing themselves. They have thick faces, not thin faces." (Dirty Trick 81 is *Thick Face, Black Heart.*) One of the reasons this is an under-used Weapon in the U.S. is because so many Americans, big dogs and guerrillas alike, are so darn hard to embarrass.

Caution: Slight embarrassment works, but heavy embarrassment backfires. When it works, its great power comes from the fact that it's so unexpected.

Two Winning Guerrilla Counter-Punches

- When the person you're dealing with uses this on you, pretend you're not embarrassed (Dirty Trick 55, *Lying*). This is hard to do. For example, how would you feel if you are meeting a potential client at his house. Suppose his wife greets you at the door with her hair in curlers and no make-up? Then, your client comes in wearing a bathrobe over a T-shirt and underwear. Would you act nonchalant and continue with the meeting? Or tell him you'll come back at a more convenient time?
- We prefer *confrontation*—tell the big dog or other guerrilla, *"You're using Dirty Tricks, and I don't like it"* (Assertive 52).

Conclusion and a Look Ahead

So much for the 50 most powerful *under*-used deal-making Weapons. In Chapters 10-15, we'll talk about the 50 most powerful *over*-used Weapons. You'll see them used against you over and over, so pay special attention to the counter-punches. You'll be using them often.

PART FOUR

DONALD WAYNE HENDON'S 50 MOST POWERFUL AND *OVER*-USED TACTICAL WEAPONS: GUERRILLAS SHOULD USE THEM EVEN THOUGH THE BIG DOG WILL EXPECT THEM, SIMPLY BECAUSE THEY'RE SO POWERFUL–CHAPTERS 10-15

It's easy to see through a big dog. The 50 Weapons in Chapters 10-15 are his favorites. He knows they usually work, so he uses them a lot. He's so predictable, and this helps guerrillas such as you. But think about this: Why are these 50 Weapons used so often in the first place, by both big dogs and guerrillas? Because they work so well. They're extremely powerful. So you should use them—and you should also be prepared for them. The best way to do this is to have several counter-punches ready to use when the big dog—and another guerrilla as well—uses them on you. These six chapters have many powerful counter-punches for you to add to your arsenal of Weapons. As you read Part Four, keep these three important things in mind:

- First, even though these 50 tactical Weapons are *over*-used, remember they're very powerful.
- Second, even though the big dog may expect you to use them, remember you're a guerrilla. Guerrillas think outside the box. Most big dogs aren't as imaginative as they were when they were just big dog wanna-be's. You will soon realize you'll win a lot from the big dog by using these Weapons in an imaginative way.
- Third, you can increase your creativity by thinking like children (Preparation 4, *Overcome paralysis of not thinking fast enough by learning from children*) and by being comfortable with ambiguity (Preparation 5, *The right attitude—I've got to earn the right to learn the needs of TOS—the other side*). Re-read these two Weapons. They're both in Chapter 5. And you can get even more information about how to become more creative and thinking outside the box by going to **www. GuerrillaDon.com.**

Chapter 10 covers two of the 50 most powerful and *over*-used tactical Weapons—two Preparation Weapons. And here's what's in Chapter 11-15:

- Chapter 11 discusses 27 Assertive Weapons—*over*-used and powerful.
- Chapter 12—12 Defensive Weapons.
- Chapter 13—three Submissive Weapons.
- Chapter 14—two Cooperative Weapons.
- Chapter 15—four Dirty Tricks.

Let's get started with the two most powerful and *over*-used preparation Weapons in Chapter 10.

CHAPTER 10

TWO PREPARATION WEAPONS— POWERFUL AND *OVER*-USED

hat this chapter is all about: Concession-making and when to reveal your demands.

Preparation Tactic 19: How to Make Concessions: 20 Do's and 20 Don'ts

Everybody makes concessions, so it's an overused Weapon. But the 40 do's and don'ts are too long to discuss here. So we've put the details in Chapter 17. Yes, concession-making is that important a tactic, and it deserves a separate chapter. Please go there for details. Read the counter-punches here.

Winning Guerrilla Counter-Punches

When the other guy makes a concession, you can either make one yourself or stick firmly to your position. What you do depends on what he concedes, your resources, and what your goals are. So there are many counter-punches— more than 100. There is one specific piece of advice we can give you here: Most negotiators don't keep careful records of what they and the other person concede. We said this back in Chapter 7. So keep records and figure out the other guy's concession patterns. And when you suspect the big dog or other guerrilla is trying to figure out *your* concession patterns, here's what you can do: Go back to Chapter 7 and use the six counter-punches you read about there. They include the following Weapons: Assertive 1 and 16. Defensive 15, 20, and 53. And Dirty Trick 55. Specifically, be ambiguous and unpredictable, show pain when you concede, watch the timing of his concessions, and observe his body language.

Preparation Weapon 23: Show Me Yours, Then I'll Show You Mine

Remember *Know Your Enemy and Know Yourself—Knowledge Is Power* (Assertive Weapon 32) in Chapter Six? Remember *Complete, Total Silence* (Defensive Weapon 10) in Chapter 7? Both you and the big dog are thinking the same thing: "I have to know what the other guy wants. I can't let him know what I want—not yet, anyway. I'll have the advantage if he goes first." This is a pissing contest in reverse. Call it a staring contest, if you want. The object is to hide important information from the other guy as long as you can. Whoever opens his mouth first is making a concession without getting one in return. And that's just plain stupid.

Let's say you want the big dog seller to give you his lowest price. You're in his office and you say to him, "I've been looking around, and I can get this at Acme Company for less than what you're asking. I'd like to buy it from you instead, so please tell me what's the best price you can give me." The big dog will probably tell you, "What price did Acme quote?" You stand firm and repeat your question. The pissing-staring contest begins. Will he break down and give you a lower price? It depends on how much he wants your business. He'll consider such things as how good a customer have you been in the past, the probability of repeat sales to you, and so forth.

He might press you further by asking you for documentation—perhaps a written bid from Acme, an ad, Acme's catalog, etc. The pissing-staring contest continues. What can you do about it?

Three Winning Guerrilla Counter-Punches

Simply refusing to tell him Acme's price without giving a reason (Assertive 71, *Be stubborn—say* no) will probably make things worse. Here's what you should do instead:

- Be firm. Tell the big dog, "I don't want to tell you what Acme's selling price is because I don't want to jeopardize my relationship with them. You can understand that, can't you?" Use Defensive Weapon 3 (*Use TOS's sense of ethics, justice, and morality*). (TOS stands for the other side.)

- Tell him "I wish I could tell you, but my hands are tied. Company policy won't let me." This is Defensive 31 (*Be overly bureaucratic*). But this isn't very believable. You've got to be a good actor—or a good liar—for this to work. Are you? *Obvious lying, not just exaggerated big talk is Dirty Trick 55.*

Then let's say he *calls your bluff* (Assertive 51) and tells you, "I don't believe you. I know Acme. Their costs are higher than ours. They can't possibly offer you the same quality merchandise at a lower price." How will you respond? We think this is the best way:

Make him feel guilty by saying, "I'm surprised at you. How can you doubt my word after all these years of doing business with you?" This is powerful Assertive Weapon 80, *Intimidate TOS by making him feel guilty.*

CHAPTER 11

27 ASSERTIVE WEAPONS–
POWERFUL AND *OVER*-USED

What this chapter is all about: *Playing dumb, astonishment, when to make your best offer, eager beavers and buyer's remorse, deadlines, blind spots, divide and conquer, arrogance, ego, good guy-bad guy, decoys, big pot, bluffing, wish lists-reality lists, charm, inside information, pressure and momentum, when to walk away, when to accept a* **no**, *the withdrawal test, intimidation (three Weapons), put the big dog on the defensive, nibble away, let's look at the record, and interrelated problems—my, ours, and yours.*

Assertive Weapon 11: Playing Dumb Is Smart. Say "Who, Me? Sorry, I Didn't Know"

It's smart to know when you're stupid. It's even smarter to know when the person you're trying to make a deal with is acting stupid on purpose. There are two ways both big dogs and guerrillas use this Weapon:

- First, they take the initiative. They do something that's to their advantage, even if it's against the unspoken, generally agreed-upon norms of negotiating. When you confront them about it, they act ignorant—they pretend they didn't know any better.

- Another way they use this is to ask you a question even when they already know the answer. Why? To test your honesty or to verify the accuracy of the information they have. Or to see if you stall by using "Who, me?"

Three Winning Guerrilla Counter-Punches

- *Watch the other guy's body language* (Defensive 15). If you're skilled at reading other people's body language, you'll be able to tell when the big dog or other guerrilla acts *too* ignorant. If this happens, watch out. He's probably just testing you.
- Be careful what you tell him. Remember—any information you give him may be used against you. You've given him part of your power without getting anything in return. And that's very, very stupid (Defensive 42, *Don't give TOS very important information*). (Please remember, TOS stands for the other side.)
- Always keep your guard up. Act on your suspicions—learn more about him. Find out if he uses this Weapon often (Defensive 22, *Get and verify information—detect and expose bullshit*).

Assertive Weapon 15: Act Astonished!

We've seen this one used by both big dogs and guerrillas alike. It usually works better for guerrillas, though. You can use it when you're buying and when you're selling. Let's say you're buying: The seller tells you what price he wants. Act astonished, but do more than just use words. Use your *body language* (Defensive 16). Be a good actor and pretend you're in pain (Assertive 16, *Show pain when you concede*).

Don uses this a lot when he's shopping in third-world countries. Shopkeepers think he's a rich Americano, and they usually ask for a lot more than they would normally get. Instead of acting like a big dog Americano, he goes into his guerrilla act. He not only yells *"Aieeee!"* but shows pain on his face. This really puts the shopkeepers off-balance. This works very well overseas, but not as well in the U.S. Acting astonished works much better than laughing at the other person's offer. This means don't use Dirty Trick 31 (*Humiliate and ridicule TOS*).

Four Winning Guerrilla Counter-Punches

- Don't believe his act (Preparation 7, *Become hard to convince*). Resist giving in.
- Whether you're buying, or selling, ask him probing questions to find out why he doesn't like what you're offering (Defensive 41, *Keep asking for more and more information*).
- Don't tell him *why* you have made the offer you did (Defensive 42, *Don't give TOS very important info*).
- Why not? Because giving away information is a big concession. Never make a concession without getting something in return (Preparation 19, *How to make concessions: 20 do's and 20 don'ts*).

Assertive Weapon 19: Don't Give the Big Dog Your Best Offer Too Soon

Don't commit yourself too early. Instead, let the big dog think you're going to give him everything he has asked for. Then, at the last minute, instead of doing what he expects you're going to do, come up with such an attractive proposal that he'll accept it and forget about his previous demands. In other words, he'll give you another concession. That's guerrilla deal-making at its best. Here are three ways you can do this:

- Tell the seller, "I'll double the size of the order if you sell at the price I want."
- Tell the seller, "I'll accept deliveries from you in your slow season. This will let you smooth out your production schedule."
- Tell the buyer, "I know you're short of cash. If you accept my offer, I'll accelerate my payment rate."

This is called *trumping his ace* in the card game Bridge.

Three Winning Guerrilla Counter-Punches

Suppose the big dog tries this on you. What would you do? It's hard to even think of counterpunches when he's being so agreeable. Nevertheless, here are three things you should think about doing and one you should not even think of:

- *Don't accept his offer too soon* (Assertive 24).

- Be skeptical (Preparation 7, *Become hard to convince*).
- Buy time by telling him, "Wow, this is so unexpected. I've got to check with my boss about this first." This is Dirty Trick 5 (*Limited authority—but first, I have to ask my mommy*).
- Finally, never make more promises to him in return, even though *promises are easier to give than concessions.* Promising him things will only make the big dog greedy for more concessions from you. In other words, don't use Cooperative 13 (*Make tempting promises instead of conceding*).

Assertive Weapon 24: Avoid Buyer's Remorse— Don't Accept His First Offer too Quickly

Guerrillas like to act quickly. It comes naturally. But don't be an eager beaver. Never accept the big dog's first offer too quickly. Even if it's so good that it gives you everything you wanted—and more. If you accept his first offer too quickly and without any haggling, two bad things will probably happen, one on the buyer's side, and one on the seller's side:

- If you're a buyer: You'll think right away that something's wrong with what you bought. You'll start resenting the seller. And you'll feel guilty about accepting too soon.
- If you're a seller: You'll think you gave away too much, and you'll start trying to get out of the deal—the sooner, the better.

Both buyers and sellers feel remorse. But for some reason, the term *buyer's remorse* has been applied to both buyers and sellers. Don't confuse this with a similar term, *winner's curse,* which pertains to competitive bidding. Because the high bidder usually overestimates the item's value, there's a good chance he overpaid. When he finds out, he'll regret it.

Four Winning Guerrilla Counter-Punches

The two most important counter-punches:

- Be skeptical and ask yourself, "Why is this person making me such a good offer, one that's too good to be true? He's not stupid. Maybe he's just trying to keep me from talking to his competitors and won't make good on his offer. Or maybe something's wrong with his product or service." This is Preparation Weapon 7 (*Become hard to convince*).

- This feeling will increase after you buy it. So avoid your own buyer's remorse by controlling your urge to buy right away. Say "I've got to think about this for a while." This is Defensive 27 (*Stall for time—get lost for a while*).

Here are two other things you can do:

- Use your *body language* to show him you're not really that interested (Defensive 16).
- Tell him, "This sounds good, but I've got to check with my boss first." This is Dirty Trick 5 (*Limited authority*).

Assertive Weapon 28: Use Deadlines Wisely

Chapter 17, *Guerrilla Concession-Making*, discusses deadlines in depth. Right now, here's a short preview. Remember these three things:

- There are many versions of the well-known 80-20 rule. Here, the 80-20 rule means this: 80 percent of the serious action in deal-making takes place in the 20 percent of the time left before the deadline. So avoid the temptation to give away too much needlessly as your deadline approaches.
- If the big dog's deadline is negotiable, he's not serious about it.
- Don't worry about his deadline. His deadline limits *his* flexibility, not *yours.* So let *him* worry about it. He has to defend it, not you. You're a lot more flexible without a deadline! Once you know his deadline, he will have more trouble with it than you have with your deadline, which you should always keep hidden.

Four Winning Guerrilla Counter-Punches

If the big dog or another guerrilla tries to find out your deadline, here are two things you can do:

- In almost all cases, don't let him know your deadline. Two Weapons here: Assertive 28 (*Use deadlines wisely*) and Defensive 42 (*Don't give*

TOS very important info). You give away too much of your power when you reveal your deadline—without getting anything in return from him. That's pretty dumb. And then, he'll probably do nothing but *stall* (Defensive 27). Then, just before your deadline, he'll *put pressure on you* (Dirty Trick 66), trying to get as many concessions from you as possible.

- The only time you should let him know your deadline is if you're using this as a take-it-or-leave-it *ultimatum* (Assertive 67). But be careful. This often backfires. He'll probably think you're under a lot of pressure to make a deal with him. And that will make him want more.

And here's how you can find out more about the other person's deadline:

- Test his deadline to see if it's legitimate or not. See if there's a cushion or not (Defensive 22, *Get and verify info*).
- Find out if his deadline is acceptable to his boss and to all third parties. If so, then it's probably legitimate. Two weapons here: Defensive 22 again. And Assertive 32 (*Knowledge is power*).

Assertive Weapon 31: Detect the Big Dog's Blind Spots and Take Advantage of Them

Before you deal with the big dog, know as much about him as possible (Assertive 32 again). If you don't know much, *watch his body language* (Defensive 15) and *listen carefully* to his words (Cooperative 14). You'll soon know what he *doesn't* know about himself. This is important information for you. Here are four guidelines to use after you learn his blind spots:

- If he's vain, flatter him. Big dogs are *much* vainer than guerrillas.
- If he's cheap, let him know what a bargain you're offering him.
- If he jumps to conclusions, make sure he reaches the conclusion you want him to reach.
- If he's afraid of making decisions, make them for him.

In other words, if he's stupid, show no mercy—take advantage of him.

Three Winning Guerrilla Counter-Punches

First, err on the side of caution—don't make snap judgments about the big dog and the other guerrilla you're dealing with. You may *think* you know when they have blind spots, but most people are wrong about this. Other people's blind spots are pretty hard to figure out. Remember what Preparation Weapon 15 said: *Prepare, trust your instincts, then do it.* But trust your instincts only if you have a winning track record.

Second, do you know *your own* blind spots? If you don't, big dogs and other guerrillas will take advantage of you, and you won't know what's happening. Here's what you should do:

- Be realistic—thoroughly know yourself, warts and all. Jay and Don have found over the years that the biggest blind spot most guerrillas, including you, have is being too optimistic. Be realistic, not an optimist. In other words, avoid Defensive Weapon 63 at all costs (*Ignore realities, concentrate on unrealistic possibilities instead*). Instead, use Assertive 32 (*Know your enemy and know yourself*).

- Then, try and get rid of all of *your* blind spots. This is going to be hard to do. You're probably not very good at recognizing your own blind spots, so err on the side of caution when making judgments about the big dog's *blind spots* (Preparation 9).

Assertive Weapon 35: Stay Powerful—Divide and Conquer

Many big dogs like to use teams when they negotiate with guerrillas. Outnumbering the other side is a strong intimidation Weapon. So when you're dealing with the big dog's team, look for the people who are most interested in what you have to say. This is easy if you know *body language* (Defensive 15). Concentrate on those people. Convince them and get them on your side. They'll help you to sell your ideas to the rest of their team.

But how do you convince them? If you're a good negotiator, simply spending more time with them than with other members of the team will often do the trick. But don't spend *too* much time with them. You don't want to alienate them from the rest of their team.

Three Winning Guerrilla Counter-Punches

- When you bring a team with you, don't let people on the other side pick off one or more members of your team and convert them. Be especially watchful. Caucus often with your team. Closely watch those who you think may be overly sympathetic to the other side's proposal. Keep them close, keep them loyal (Assertive 54, *Control the agreement process*).
- If that's hard to do, withdraw for a while, but continue working behind the scenes to accomplish your goals (Dirty Trick 56, *Lie about withdrawing—you're still there, hiding behind intermediaries*).
- If all else fails, impose communication limits on your team members (Assertive 55, *Limit what your team can tell TOS*).

Assertive Weapon 38: Act Arrogant—Overwhelm the Person You're Dealing With by Pulling Rank

This is Assertiveness to the extreme, and it fits in with everything big dogs and big dog wanna-be's stand for. You see this everywhere:

- In the military, officers use this on enlisted men (Assertive 86, *Intimidate TOS with lawful, legitimate power*).
- Traffic cops use it on speeders (Assertive 86 again).
- Pompous clergymen seem to use it with everybody (Dirty Trick 26, *Phony sanctimony*). Ditto *celebrities* (Assertive 95) and politicians.
- Bosses use this on their employees (Assertive 90, *Intimidate TOS by your status in the company*).
- And big dogs with big egos use it on almost everybody. They seem to especially enjoy intimidating guerrillas.

Our advice: Use this Weapon in moderation. Don't bully your opponent with it. You may not be as powerful as you think you are, especially if you have a big *blind spot* (Preparation 9). Never use it in anger. But if you don't want to negotiate with him, go ahead and use it. Say something like, "Who do you think you are, anyway, challenging me like this?"

Six Winning Guerrilla Counter-Punches

Don't let the big dog intimidate you. In fact, if you have any of these five characteristics, you can pull rank on the big dog yourself. So use this Weapon to your advantage:

- You have a prestigious occupation (doctor, university professor). But be careful—your occupation may be a lot less prestigious than you think. For example, the Harris Poll says the general public think being a fireman is more prestigious than being a member of the U.S. Congress (Assertive 92, *Intimidate TOS by your prestigious occupation*).
- You are an acknowledged expert in your field—better yet, you're a *well-known* expert (Assertive 94, *Intimidate TOS by your expertise*).
- You are a *celebrity* (Assertive 95).
- You are his boss (Assertive 90, *Intimidate TOS by your status in the company*).
- You are sleeping with his boss (Assertive 93, *Intimidate TOS by being untouchable*).

If you don't have any of these characteristics and really want to make a deal with an intimidating big dog, bring in a well-known expert, and let him negotiate for you (Assertive 3, *Surprise TOS with your expert*).

Assertive Weapon 39: Act Egotistical—I'm the Greatest!

Use this when you want to lower the big dog's expectations. He might accept less from you than he thinks he can get because he's dealing with a *superstar*. So impress him with your accomplishments, especially if they're recent. Old accomplishments aren't impressive. He wants to know "What have you done lately?"

There are three bad things about using it:

- If you're trying to con him (Dirty Trick 55, *Obvious lying, not just exaggerated big talk*), he might see through you.
- If you're simply bragging, he may be turned off by your big ego (Dirty Trick 2, *Get an invulnerable reputation—you brag, get others to brag about you*).

- If he believes you, he might want more from you, ask for more, and even get more, especially if you have a *Santa Claus* mentality (Assertive 85, *I can afford to give it away*).

Three Winning Guerrilla Counter-Punches

When big dogs and other guerrillas act like they're the greatest, here's what you can do to burst their bubble and bring them down to earth:

- Check out their claims to see if they're lying to you or not—and let them know you're doing this (Defensive 22, *Get and verify information—detect and expose bullshit*).
- Negotiate on the basis of *issues*, not on the razzle-dazzle of *presentations* (Assertive 33, *Be logical—and make sure TOS knows you are*).
- Control your ego. Don't get into a pissing contest with him to determine who's greater (Preparation 10, *Deal with your ego*).

Assertive Weapon 44: Good Guy, Bad Guy

Everybody knows this one. Along with *Decoy* (Assertive 47) and *Big Pot* (Assertive 48), these are the three most widely used deal-making Weapons of all—used by big dogs and guerrillas alike. But even though all three are overdone, each of them works. In fact, they work very well. That's why they're used so often.

When the other side uses this Weapon against you, they'll always negotiate as a two-person team. That's a dead give-away. The one playing the bad guy acts unreasonable during the first session, while the one playing the good guy keeps a quiet, reasonable profile. The bad guy finds some excuse to leave the room. While he's gone, the good guy tells you, "I can get my partner to do better than that. I'm really on *your* side, not on *his* side. He's just an asshole." When you use it, heed this caution: It's very easy for anybody to spot this Weapon, even if both of you are good actors.

Three Winning Guerrilla Counter-Punches
- *Call their bluff* (Assertive 51). Confront them by looking both of them in the eye and saying, "Wow, that's the best good guy-bad guy act I've ever seen. I've got to learn how to do that." Or groan and say, "Gee, that's the worst good guy-bad guy act I've ever seen."

- Smile when you groan. Doing this shows them you're not upset about it (Cooperative 24, *Ooze warmth, but try to appear sincere about it*).
- Never use Assertive Weapon 14—*Pretending you believe their act*. If you try to make them think you really believe what they're trying to pull on you, they'll assume you're stupid, and they'll try to take even more advantage of you than they have already. So don't go along with their charade.

Assertive Weapon 47: Use a *Decoy* to Divert Attention from What You *Really* Want

How good an actor are you? You've got to be very, very good, because this Weapon is easy to spot. You've done this yourself many times—you throw into the pot some low-priority objectives (the Decoy) along with your high-priority objectives (the real ones). You lie and try to make the big dog or other guerrilla think your low-priority objectives are very important to you. Then, when the time comes, give some or all of these low priorities away—but don't give up what you *really* want. In other words, destroy the decoy, keep the real objectives.

Three Winning Guerrilla Counter-Punches

When the big dog or another guerrilla tries this on you, here's what you can do about it:

- *Confront TOS—call his bluff* (Assertive 51). Tell him know you know he's *lying* (Dirty Trick 55).
- Use your *own* decoy—see if he'll accept that as your concession, not what he *really* wants from you (Assertive 47).
- Finally, if he persists and you don't really want to give in to him, simply walk away from the deal (Assertive 68, *Say "Take it or leave it—Elvis has left the building"*).

Assertive Weapon 48: Size Matters—the Big Pot

This is so obvious: If you're a buyer, start low. If you're a seller, start high. Give yourself a lot of room to negotiate. Make many demands at the beginning. Perhaps unrealistically high demands. Even after you make several concessions, you'll still probably end up with a bigger payoff than if you started off too low.

Big dogs and other guerrillas *expect* you to use it. Don't disappoint them—use this Weapon. It's all part of the deal-making game. If you don't use it, they'll won't respect you or think you're a liar. Or think you're just plain stupid and naïve.

Five Winning Guerrilla Counter-Punches

Try our any of these five counter-punches, and then pick the ones which work best for you. Use them at the appropriate time:

- Tell him he's being unrealistic and he's *gotta do better than that* (Defensive 87).
- But don't insult him by calling him a liar. Use Assertive 60 (*Smooth talk, flattery, and charm*) Don't use Dirty Trick 31 (*Humiliate and ridicule TOS*).
- Laughing at his proposal in a good-natured way is probably OK, though, as long as you don't overdo it and try to *humiliate or ridicule him*. This means you should use Dirty Trick 31 with caution, especially when you deal with big dogs. Guerrillas, on the other hand, will probably admire you for being good-natured about it.
- Come up with your own *Big pot* (Assertive 48).
- This is a good time to throw as many things from your *Wish List* into your own big pot (Assertive 56).

Assertive Weapon 50: Bluffing: Not-Too-Obvious Lying

Deal-makers bluff about many things—how much money they have, their deadlines, their knowledge, their credentials, and so forth. Bluffing is lying, but this kind of a lie is *expected* in deal-making. And because it's expected, you don't have to be a good actor to bluff. In fact, if you *don't* bluff, both big dogs and guerrillas will think you're weak and will try and take advantage of you. Our advice: Go ahead and bluff. But be as believable as possible when you do.

And here's something a lot of deal-makers overlook: The *threat* of a bluff is just as important as a bluff itself—good poker players know this.

Two Winning Guerrilla Counter-Punches

- *Call his bluff* if it's to your advantage (Assertive 51).

- And when you call his bluff, let him know you don't even care that he's bluffing. Tell him "So what?" This shows you have less commitment to the relationship than he does, and this gives you *a lot* more power (Defensive 9, *The person with the* least *commitment to the relationship has the* most *power*).

Assertive Weapon 56: Wish Lists vs. Reality Lists

You ask for so many things that the big dog or other guerrilla loses focus on his own demands. This is like using a shotgun (wide area) instead of a rifle (narrow area—more focused).

And if you don't want to overwhelm him all at once, don't tell him everything you want at once—spread your Wish List over a longer period of time (Assertive 103, *Nibble away—wear out TOS, outlast him*).

Five Winning Guerrilla Counter-Punches

- *Confront him* (Assertive 51). Our deal-making experience tells us that there are very seldom more than four major issues in a negotiation. If the big dog wants to talk about more than four things, tell him "You're just giving me your wish list. Let me have your reality list instead."
- But don't be confrontational. Make your request with a knowing smile so he knows you think he's not really being serious with you (Cooperative 24, *Ooze warmth, but try hard to appear sincere about it*).
- Ask him to prioritize his long list (Preparation 3—*Set priorities using the 80-20 rule*).
- Come up with your own wish list. That's a good counter-attack. Two weapons here: Assertive 56 (*Wish list*) and Defensive 90 (*Debate no; counter-attack yes*).
- If his wish list has caught you by surprise, ask for a recess so you can have time to think (Defensive 27, *Stall for time—get lost for a while*).

Assertive Weapon 60: Use Smooth Talk, Charm, and Flattery

Learn from the sweet talk we all use when we flirt. In deal-making, you need to feed the other person's ego, too, especially if he's a big dog. If he thinks you're sincere, this might make him swap his *negotiating* needs for his *ego* needs.

Example: "You're the best speaker I know, and I need a great speaker for the charity fund-raising event. But I don't have any money in my budget to pay you. Will you speak?" Would *you* fall for this?

Four Winning Guerrilla Counter-Punches

- Say "I know I'm a great speaker. That's why I don't give away my talent for free." Two weapons here: Assertive 39 (*Act arrogant—I'm the greatest!*) and Assertive 71 (*Be stubborn—say* no).
- In a nice way, tell the big dog, "What can you offer me besides money? And don't tell me I'll impress lots of people at the event who will later become my clients. I've heard that one before." This is Assertive Weapon 62 (*Exaggerate slightly, but not too much*).
- Let's get back to flirting. All over the world, women seem to be the pursued, and men are almost always the pursuers. Many women respond to flattery by making themselves even more desirable. They do this by *making men aware of their competition* (Defensive 4). And if they don't have a suitor, they'll make one up (Dirty Trick 55, *Obvious lying, not just exaggerated big talk*).

Assertive Weapon 61: Convince the Big Dog You Have Lots of General Information, Even if You Don't

Put up a false front. Make sure you make the big dog or the other guerrilla think you have a lot more information than you really do. And not just info about him and his company. How? Here are five ways:

- Act confident (Assertive 39, *Act egotistical—I'm the greatest*).
- *Dress well* (Assertive 42).
- *Use your body language* to manipulate him (Defensive 16).
- If your credentials are powerful, like a Ph.D., use them (Assertive 91, *Intimidate TOS by your credentials*).
- And make sure you plan ahead so you'll know what to do if he asks you for that information you're only pretending to have (Preparation 2, *Pick your battles carefully—prepare, rehearse, manage your time*). If you're a bad actor, he'll see through you right away.

Three Winning Guerrilla Counter-Punches

- If you have contacts in his company, use them to find out if he really knows what he's talking about or if he's just a liar (Defensive 76, *Find allies and use them*).
- *Watch his body language* to see if he's lying or not (Defensive 15).
- If you think he's lying, *call his bluff* (Assertive 51).

Assertive Weapon 66: Momentum: Always Keep Pressure on the Big Dog and the Other Guerrilla

This is *extremely* assertive, and it almost always works—on big dogs and guerrillas alike. Here, you want to develop an unstoppable momentum. How can you do this? Three ways:

- Take the initiative right from the start.
- Be forceful on the issues you're discussing.
- Move steadily and firmly toward your objectives.

You may be thinking, "Doing this might lead to conflict with the guy I'm trying to make a deal with. I don't think I'm going to use this Weapon after all." We say don't be afraid of conflict. Conflict can actually be healthy, if it's a *mild* degree of conflict. You should welcome *mild* conflict. If you try to avoid even the *smallest* conflict at all costs, you'll get stressed out, and your ability to get what you want from big dogs and other guerrillas goes way, way down.

So don't get stressed out, especially when you're trying to make a deal. Too much stress is unhealthy. There are 45 bad things that can happen to you if you're under too much stress—18 effects on your body, 17 effects on your thoughts and feelings, and 10 effects on your behavior. From high blood pressure to decreased productivity. Too much stress makes you a less effective as a deal-maker. You can read about them in Chapter Two of Don's book, *365 Powerful Ways to Negotiate*. Or go to **www.GuerrillaDon.com**. The website gives you information about how to handle conflict and stress, right out of Don's seminar on the subject.

Six Winning Guerrilla Counter-Punches

- Stay firm and don't let the big dog's pressure tactics affect you. Two Weapons here: Assertive 71 (*Be stubborn—say* no). And Defensive 89 (*Don't give in to unreasonable demands*).

- Check his position closely and often. It may change. If you're a good deal-maker, he will address your needs and objectives eventually. Two Weapons again: Assertive 32 (*Know your enemy and know yourself—knowledge is power*). And Defensive 22 (*Get and verify information*).

- Think of this as an opportunity to size up the other person under conditions of heavy, stressful bargaining. The big dog might be hard as nails, or he might turn out to be a pussycat. *Watching his body language* (Defensive 15) will tell you how much stress he's under—or how little.

- *Listening carefully* to his voice can tell you this, too (Cooperative 14). Does his voice crack? Does he suddenly start to stammer or ramble? If so, he's under stress.

- Never let him think you're under pressure. Always act cool and confident. Two weapons: Preparation 31 (*When you do things right, people won't be sure you did anything at all*). And Assertive 41 (Imply *your power—don't intentionally* display *it*).

- Whether you're dealing with big dogs or other guerrillas, *make them aware of their competition*—make sure they know you can go elsewhere to get what you want. This is a very effective counter-punch (Defensive 4).

Assertive 68: Say "Take It or Leave It" and be Prepared to Walk Away—Elvis Has Left the Building

Give the big dog or the other guerrilla only one firm choice. If he doesn't accept your offer, tell him "No deal." See what he does. If he doesn't budge, simply walk away. If you want to be sarcastic and have nothing to lose, tell him, "Elvis has left the building" as you're leaving. But don't give him the finger on your way out. That's not only rude, it's counter-productive. Most deal-makers use "No deal" as a *bluff* (Assertive 50). It's a short cut to get the other guy to move closer to your desired position.

Deal-makers also use it on purpose to deadlock negotiations which no longer hold any promise—a slow but sure way of killing it, in other words. So if all else fails and you're not interested in building a long-term relationship with the other guy, use it as a last resort and get out.

Six Winning Guerrilla Counter-Punches

Arrogant big dogs use this a lot. Most guerrillas use this as a last resort. No matter who uses it on you, don't let them him think he can manipulate you with this over-used tactic. Here are six ways to do this:

- Ignore what he said (Defensive 11, *Don't react at all*).
- Maybe even pretend you didn't hear him (Assertive 100, *Ignore TOS—have a deaf ear*).
- Use *funny money* (Defensive 6). In other words, use percentages instead of dollars. Somehow, percentages make the amount of money involved seem smaller.
- *Remind him of his competition* (Defensive 4).
- Use your creativity to come up with unique ways of breaking the deadlock (Preparation 4, *Overcome paralysis of not thinking fast enough by learning from children*).
- Firmly re-define your position in reasonable terms (Assertive 102, *Be flexibly persistent*).

Assertive Weapon 72: Never Accept a No from the Big Dog or Another Guerrilla

When the big dog or another guerrilla tells you *no*, think of it as a threat to the achievement of your objectives. That's why you should never accept his *no*. But be careful how you tell him that his *no* is unacceptable.

And be especially careful about threatening him in retaliation. Don't give in to that temptation. Always remember that you can use threats *only once* in a relationship and still remain credible.

Here's another thing to think about: The big dog or the other guerrilla may just be testing your resolve by continually turning you down. Don't let him win the test.

Four Winning Guerrilla Counter-Punches

When the other person tells you *no*, here's what you can do:

- Make sure he knows you're *getting ready to walk out* (Assertive 73).
- If he keeps on arguing with you after you say his *no* is unacceptable to you, then go ahead and walk away (Assertive 68, *Say "Take it or leave it"*). If you don't do this, you'll lose all credibility.
- But walk away only if you're less committed to the relationship than he is (Defensive 9, *The person with the* least *commitment to the relationship has the* most *power*).
- Finally, if you decide not to walk away after all, you've got to be creative enough to come up with an alternative that will make TOS move away from his position (Preparation 4, *Overcome paralysis of not thinking fast enough by learning from children*).

Sometimes, you need to use threats. The next Weapon is a pretty good threat to use:

Assertive Weapon 73: Tell the Big Dog or the Other Guerrilla You're Getting Ready to Withdraw from the Deal

There are four ways to do this. From strongest to weakest, they are:

- Tell the big dog, "We aren't getting anywhere. I don't see the point of continuing this. Contact me if you change your mind." Then, get off your chair and walk toward the door if you're in *his* office, or ask him to leave if he's in *your* office. If he says, "Wait a minute," and tries to stop you, then you know he needs the deal more than you do—and that means you're more powerful. Exploit your power.
- Tell him, "It's a shame that we both wasted each other's time for so long. I don't feel like continuing this any longer."
- Say, "I'm leaving unless you bring in a different negotiator."
- And you may want to think about bringing in another negotiator on *your* side. You say, "You and I have reached a deadlock. Perhaps other people can resolve this issue. We sure can't. I'll ask my company to send somebody else to talk to you."

Five Winning Guerrilla Counter-Punches and Two No-No's

Here's the first *No-No*: Never, ever say "Wait a minute," and try to stop him. You lose all your power that way.

No-no number two: When the big dog or the other guerrilla tells you he's tired and is getting ready to withdraw, don't get angry at him. That only escalates the situation. In other words, don't use Assertive Weapon 101 (*Pretend to lose your temper*) or Dirty Trick 51 (*Scare the hell out of TOS—make him fear you*).

Instead of losing your temper, ask him, "Please tell me why you're making this threat. I just don't understand." Using Assertive Weapon 11 (*Playing dumb is smart*) is the best thing you can do.

And if you have a good reason for not wanting to do this, here are four other things you can try:

- Get the support of people in his company. They may be able to persuade him to be more reasonable (Defensive 76, *Find allies and use them*).

- Ignore his threat. Don't get emotional. In fact, don't do anything at all. Let it happen (Defensive 11, *Don't react at all, either positively or negatively*).

- On the other hand, *get and verify information* (Defensive 22). Find out if he's threatening to break off negotiations just to make you look bad in the eyes of your boss. If that's his reason and if you're already in trouble with your boss, you probably should make a serious effort to mend your relationship (Defensive 22).

- Agree with the big dog or other guerrilla. It might be a good thing to bring in a fresh face after all, especially if there are really big differences in perceptions and style which can't be reconciled. Tell him, "Well, since you're bringing in a different negotiator, I'll do the same thing." Two weapons here: Assertive 73 (*Tell TOS you're getting ready to withdraw from the deal.*) and Submissive 6, *Don't argue—turn the other cheek instead*).

Assertive Weapon 78: Intimidate Big Dogs and Other Guerrillas by Tradition, Custom, and Conformity

Limit your room to negotiate a deal. Do this on purpose. Simply say, "That's the way we do things at our company." Use this Weapon when you want to set up a barrier as to how far big dogs or other guerrillas can push you. Some people are intimidated by this. Others aren't. Here's how to predict that the other guy will probably be intimidated if you try this on him:

- He always wears a suit and tie, even on Casual Fridays. He does this even though he's uncomfortable wearing them.
- Women negotiators who are afraid to be anything else but passive and feminine are definitely intimidated.

And if you're dealing with the other person for the first time, here's a clue that he'll probably pull this tactical Weapon on you before you complete the deal:

- He tells you, "It's unthinkable to work on the day our company was founded. It's always been a holiday."

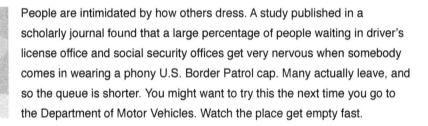

People are intimidated by how others dress. A study published in a scholarly journal found that a large percentage of people waiting in driver's license office and social security offices get very nervous when somebody comes in wearing a phony U.S. Border Patrol cap. Many actually leave, and so the queue is shorter. You might want to try this the next time you go to the Department of Motor Vehicles. Watch the place get empty fast.

Five Winning Guerrilla Counter-Punches

Warning: Guerrillas usually think outside the box, so they tend to ignore this Weapon when it's used against them (Defensive 11, *Don't react at all*). *Never ignore this intimidation Weapon!*

So when the big dog uses it against you, remember this—he's probably intimidated himself and thinks everybody should be, including you. He'll be suspicious of you if you don't share his values. So be careful about what counter-punches you use. Try these:

- Mimic not only his body language, but also his clothing (Defensive 16, *Manipulate TOS with your own body language*).
- Develop sources within his company to see if he's telling you the truth or not. Three weapons here: Defensive 76 (*Find allies and use them*).

Defensive 22 (*Get and verify information—detect and expose bullshit*). And Assertive 32 (*Knowledge is power*).

- If he's not telling you the truth, there are two things you can do: Either *confront* him (Assertive 52), or give in and take what he offers you (Submissive 16, *Accept defeat*). We've had better results using confrontation instead of submission, but it's up to you to determine what would work best in your particular deal-making situation.

Assertive Weapon 80: Intimidate the Big Dog by Making Him Feel Guilty

When big dogs or other guerrillas do something negative without being aware of it, look upon this as an opportunity to make them feel guilty, especially if you've done favors for them in the past. But before you use any harsh *guilt trip* words, give them the chance to realize what they've done and to apologize to you. After all, they may have hurt you without even knowing it. So if you have a good relationship with them and want it to continue, give them a chance to review what happened. After they do that, if they don't care about what they did to you, then pull out your big guns. Put them on a *heavy guilt trip* with these intimidating words:

- I'm surprised at you.
- Shame on you.
- How can you do this to me after all I've done for you over the years? Don's mother often used this version on him when he was a teenager: "How can you treat me so bad, after I carried you in my womb for nine months, was sick the entire time, and went through 30 hours of labor giving birth to you?" He finally got her to stop by saying, "Sorry, mom, I promise you this: You'll never have to do that with me again."

There's a big *but* here: Using intimidating words might end the chance of ever reaching an agreement with the big dog or the other guerrilla. Think about it. Is this what you *really* want?

Three Winning Guerrilla Counter-Punches

Trying to make you feel guilty by implying nothing you do ever pleases him is nothing more than the big dog's power play. He's nothing more than a control freak. He *wants* you to feel guilty—not only does that make him feel good inside, it also gives him more power over you. If you're dealing with that kind of a person, here's what you can do:

- We suggest you walk out (Assertive 68, *Elvis has left the building*). And don't feel guilty about walking out.
- But if you're a masochist (Submissive 15, *Self-destruction—see me, catch me, stop me, save me*) and want to continue this charade, keep it going by *reminding him of his competition* (Defensive 4).
- Finally, *pick your deal-making targets better* (Preparation 2). Don't waste your time on these kinds of self-righteous people who put you on a *guilt trip* just to make them feel better about themselves. They only want to feed their ego—they're not that interested in making a deal with you.

Assertive Weapon 88: Intimidate the Big Dog by Rewarding Him or Punishing Him

You learned this Weapon way back when you were a kid. You still remember what your parents told you: "If you don't clean up your room, no TV for a week." Later on, your boss arbitrarily set your quota much too high and told you, "If you don't meet your quota, you're fired." And there are so many power-mad big dogs out there who think giving you a concession is just like throwing a bone to a dirty dog.

You've used this Weapon many times before. But have you used it the right way? You have to be careful when you use it. If it gets the big dog or the other guerrilla—whoever you're negotiating with—angry at you, watch out! When that happens, your deal-making session will be on a downward spiral that will be hard to reverse. So don't be heavy-handed. It's much better to be subtle (Defensive 53, *Use creative vagueness*).

Three Winning Guerrilla Counter-Punches

If he's using reward-punishment as a threat, here are three things you can do:

- *Call his bluff* (Assertive 51). How? By making him know you don't like it, especially if you feel you're being treated unjustly.

- If calling his bluff doesn't work, then you should take some kind of action. *Reward or punish him* (Assertive 88). Unions do this. They go on strike even if management threatens them with immediate expulsion. Then, the company retaliates by joining with other companies. They come up with a management lockout (Defensive 75, *Join with others—lockouts, strikes, boycotts*).
- Or, if you think you've gotten most of what you want, you might want to think about *giving in and take whatever you can get* (Submissive 16).

Assertive Weapon 97: Put the Big Dog or the Other Guerrilla on the Defensive— Accuse Him, Make Negative Statements, and…

People who use this usually start out by making accusative questions such as "Have you stopped beating your wife yet?" Then, they turn to a series of negative statements that seem to attack you personally as well as your company. Should you use this? Only if you think the big dog is weak and will give in quickly.

But use this Weapon for brief periods only. Use other Weapons in between. Using it too often means you want to humiliate him. And if that's your purpose, why are you dealing with him in the first place? The sadistic side of your ego will rejoice, but no deal will occur.

There are many power-hungry egotists and many weak people, and that's why this Weapon is used so much. There are many spiders and many flies. Which one are you?

Five Winning Guerrilla Counter-Punches

When you don't like what the big dog or other guerrilla is telling you, here's what you can do:

- Take the low road and get angry at the other person on purpose (Dirty Trick 51, *Scare the hell out of TOS*).
- Or take the high road and say something like, "I've never beaten my wife, and I never will. I don't like you accusing me of this. Assaulting somebody is a terrible thing to do. And accusing an innocent person is also a terrible thing to do." This is Assertive Weapon 52 (*Confront TOS—Why are you using Dirty Tricks, and when will you stop*).

- No matter what you say to him, the deal almost certainly won't go through. So cut your losses and investment of time (Preparation 13, *The escalation commitment—throwing good money after bad is stupid*), and quickly walk out (Assertive 68, *Elvis has left the building*). Remember, life's too short to deal with people who want to make your life miserable.

- On the other hand, if making a deal is important to you, re-state your position *briefly* and *emphatically* (Cooperative 11, *Speak so clearly there's no chance TOS will misunderstand*). Don't over-explain or get defensive—if you do, you're walking right into his trap. And don't get into a pissing contest and try to get the last word.

- Get out of his office quickly (Assertive 68, *Elvis has left the building*). And on your way out, avoid the temptation of shouting out the last word on your way out the door.

Assertive Weapon 103: Nibble Away—Wear Out the Big Dog and the Other Guerrilla, Outlast Him

Get things, bit by bit, from the person you're dealing with. Do it so slowly that he doesn't really notice how much all of this is costing him. Eventually, you'll get everything you wanted. You won't get nearly as much if you overwhelm him with your entire *Wish List* all at once (Assertive 56). Three other Weapons you can use to overwhelm the other guy are: Assertive 57 (*Negotiate at your place*). Assertive 58 (*Tuangou / swarming ambush / flash mobs*). And 59, (*Your team is larger than their team*).

But we're not talking about overwhelming the other guy. This is about nibbling away. We all learned how to do this when we were kids. We were *flexibly persistent* (Assertive 102), we were creatively irritating (Preparation 4, *Think fast by learning from children*). We did this to test our parents, to see if the limits they imposed on us were solid or if they could be bent. We pushed them to the limit. And when we became adults, we tested our bosses this way—if we thought we could get away with it.

Creative Reciprocity: Getting Rid of Guilt

Nibbling away works so well because it's tied in with the powerful over-used Weapon of *Reciprocity* (Cooperative 4). Think of it this way: You deliberately make an extremely large request that the big dog will obviously turn down. Then you nibble away by making a more reasonable request. He'll be more likely to give in to your second request since it's not accompanied by your first ridiculously big request. In other words, turning down the big request you made first creates a sense of debt and guilt in the big dog. The debt / guilt goes away only when he agrees to your second request He gives up his sense of guilt, which makes him happy, and you get what you wanted in the first place. That's *creative* reciprocity! (We'll talk about *subtle* reciprocity in a box in Chapter 14.)

Six Winning Guerrilla Counter-Punches

When the big dog or the other guerrilla keeps on nibbling away at you, you can either keep saying *no*, or you can make a concession. If you tell him *no*, prove it to him with figures. Use Defensive Weapon 32—tell him you've reached your limit, you have no more money to give away.

And if you decide to make a concession, here are six ways to do it:

- Each time you make a concession, write down how many dollars you're giving away. Keep a running total. You'll know when you reach your limit. If he asks you why you're not giving him more concessions, show him your figures (Preparation 19, *20 do's and don'ts of concession-making*).

- Know what you're doing. Take careful notes about what *you* concede and what *he* concedes. Track your *pattern of vulnerability*. How did he get you to give in? Did you even know you gave in one of his demands? Was your concession *really* that small? Or was it a lot bigger than you thought it was? This is Preparation Weapon 19 again.

- Try logic. Let the guy you're dealing with know you've made one concession after another, and the negotiation is no longer win-win. Tell him it's become *You win, I lose* (Assertive 33, *Be logical—and make sure TOS knows you are*).

- When the big dog asks you for a particularly large concession, be a good actor. Pretend to be very, very surprised. As you read earlier in this chapter, Don likes to shout "Aieeee!" He combines this with a look of fake horror on his face and places his hands on his cheeks. All at the same time. For some reason, it works—probably because it's so outrageously transparent, it's actually funny (Assertive 15, *Act astonished*).

- And after you act surprised, try for a trade-off—get something in return for your concession. Remember, a promise is *not* a concession. Promises are easy to make, hard to keep. Two weapons here: Defensive 88 (*Use trade-offs, but don't mess with promises*). And Cooperative 13 (*Make tempting promises instead of conceding*). Chapter 17 tells you a lot more about conceding.

- Above all, be firm. Bargain harder each time you give up something (Submissive 12, *The tough give-in*).

Assertive Weapon 104: Hey, Let's Look at the Record

Prove what you're saying is correct by bringing in facts and figures. Make sure they're relevant and that they'll show the big dog or the other guerrilla how he'll benefit from these numbers. But remember, he's always going to think you're using only those facts and figures which support what you've been telling him, and he'll be right. Facts and figures won't convince him, so don't use them as a crutch. Remember, *numbers* don't negotiate. *Human beings* do. That means you've still got a big job to do.

Six Winning Guerrilla Counter-Punches

- Examine his data closely to weed out the *bullshit* factor (Defensive 22, *Get and verify information*). Be especially on the lookout for *funny money* (Defensive 6). Don't be blinded by TOS's use of small percentages—think of big dollars instead.
- Hire an expert to look over his data, especially if your negotiations involve highly technical data. It's easy to get mixed up here (Assertive 37, *Use a professional or agent to assist you in negotiating*).
- *Watch his body language* (Defensive 15). See if he's really convinced he's right when he delivers his facts to you. Or if he's lying.
- Don't let him off too easily. Make him do the work of convincing you with his arguments (Preparation 7, *Become hard to convince*).
- Tell him, "*You've gotta do better than that*" (Defensive 87) and *threaten to walk out* if he doesn't improve his offer (Assertive 73).

- Remain silent and impassive, even if he's extremely enthusiastic and talkative. Two Weapons here: Defensive 10 (*Complete, total silence*). Defensive 11 (*Don't react at all*).

Assertive Weapon 118: Turn *My* Problem into *Our* Problem, and Finally into *Your* Problem

This is so easy to spot: One of your employees tells you, "Boss, *we* have a problem." Watch out! Most of the time, this means he doesn't want to do something. He's trying to pass the buck upward to you. Customers and suppliers try this on you, too, especially if they have a long-term relationship with you and your company, and if their problem's too hot to handle.

Three Winning Guerrilla Counter-Punches

Never take on a problem of one of your business associates—unless there's a big payoff for you when you do it. On the other hand, always help somebody you care for and love deeply. If you don't want to take on his problem, try these three counter-punches:

- Tell him, "I don't have the power or authority to do this." Two weapons here: Defensive 30 (*Give TOS the run-around*). Dirty Trick 5 (*But first, I have to ask my mommy*).
- If you decide to help him out, always get something in return (Defensive 88, *Use trade-offs, but don't mess with promises*).
- Don't say, "Let me think about it." That's much too weak. It raises his expectations, and anything you do that raises somebody else's expectations is a concession. Never give a concession without getting something in return. Always say instead, "What will you do for me if I even *decide* to think about it." This is Preparation Weapon 19 (*20 do's and 20 don'ts of concession-making*).

CHAPTER 12

12 DEFENSIVE WEAPONS— POWERFUL AND *OVER*-USED

W *hat this chapter is all about: Powerlessness and creeping paralysis, reminding big dog of his competitors, funny money, expectations, forgetting on purpose, the run-around, the no money excuse, information, honesty, nagging, you gotta do better than that, and trade-offs.*

Defensive Weapon 1: The Power of Powerlessness and Creeping Paralysis

Do you often feel powerless? If so, you're not a true guerrilla at heart. Guerrillas are very powerful, even though most people think they're not because they're small. You should exploit that misperception. When you get discouraged about changing the big dog's mind, *power-up* by thinking about these 11 power sources that you probably already have. Knowing you have them makes you more confident, and when you're confident, you'll probably win more.

You're More Powerful Than You Think—Your 11 Hidden Power Sources

- Doing without. Make sure the big dog knows you can get along very well without him, his products, and his services. Remember, *the*

151

person who is least committed to the relationship has the most power.
Two defensive weapons here: Defensive 4 (*Remind the other side—TOS—of his competition*) and Defensive 9 (*The person with the* least commitment to the relationship has the most *power*).

- Your skill in making concessions (Preparation 19, *20 do's and 20 don'ts of concession-making*).
- Your skill as a negotiator. Remember, this particular skill will be even more powerful after you master the 365 Weapons in your book.
- Good intelligence-gathering. This gives you accurate knowledge about the big dog and the deal-making situation. *Knowledge definitely is power.* (Assertive 32).
- And don't forget about knowing yourself, too—being brutally honest about yourself and *getting rid of your blind spots* makes you a lot more powerful (Preparation 9).
- The power of being skeptical, not gullible. This makes you check the accuracy of what the big dog tells you (Preparation 7, *Become hard to convince*).
- Knowing how to use *deadlines*—both yours and his (Assertive 28).
- Being able to tolerate ambiguity. Embracing the wobble (Preparation 5, *I've got to earn the right to learn TOS's needs*).
- Being thoroughly prepared (Preparation 2, *Pick your battles carefully—prepare, rehearse, manage your time*).
- Being able to outwait the big dog—the *power of patience* (Cooperative 1).
- And having a good reputation as an expert in your field gives you a lot of power. If you're an expert, use it to your advantage (Assertive 94, *Intimidate TOS by your expertise or bringing an expert with you*).

Now here's Power Source 12. It's this Weapon—*The Power of Powerlessness* itself. It's one of the strongest sources of power most of us have. That's right—paradoxically, powerlessness is very, very powerful. If your position is weak—or if your position is strong and want the big dog to *think* you're weak—show him how much *he* has to lose by taking too much advantage of you. Here are two examples:

- If you don't help me, I'll go bankrupt, and you won't get anything from me. We'll both lose.
- I can't afford to pay you what you are asking to repair my transmission. Just put it back into the car, and I will call somebody and pay to tow it away to the junkyard, where I will sell the car for its parts.

There's another way many people use this power: Don calls it *Creeping paralysis.* Some call it *Calculated incompetence.* Example: Your boss pretends he doesn't know how to operate a photocopying machine. He does this to get attention from—and more power over—you.

Four Winning Guerrilla Counter-Punches

- Act skeptical—like you've heard all this many times before (Preparation 7, *Become hard to convince*). And then *call his bluff* (Assertive 51).
- Don't let the big dog or the other guerrilla think his story has any impact on you, good or bad. Sit there impassively (Defensive 11, *Don't react at all*). And don't say anything (Defensive 10, *Complete, total silence*).
- If you want to find out if he's lying or not, *watch his body language* (Defensive 15). And then try and get information from other sources to check out his story (Defensive 22, *Get and verify information— detect and expose bullshit*).
- Blame your refusal on your company. Tell him, "Sorry, but our company policy won't let me give in." This is Defensive 31 (*Be overly bureaucratic*). Or blame it on your boss. Say "My boss won't let me do this." This is Dirty Trick 5 (*But first, I have to ask my mommy*).

A Losing Power Play

Here's an imaginative power play that didn't work. Nobody's as powerless as prison inmates. But when people have nothing to lose, they try anything. In 2003, four inmates in Oklahoma copyrighted their names, sued the warden for using their names without permission, demanded several million dollars from him, and filed liens against his property. They hired somebody to seize his cars, freeze his bank accounts, and change the locks on his house. They told the warden they wouldn't return his property unless they were released from prison. We wonder how the warden punished them.

Don writes a column for his hometown newspaper, *Mesquite Local News*. One column, *Influence by Cruelty*, is about how police officers sometimes intentionally mistreat prisoners in the Clark County Detention Center in Las Vegas. Former inmates allege the ten tactics cops use the most are Assertive 38, 85, 86, 100, 112; Defensive 42; and Dirty Tricks 2, 21, 30, 50. They also use six tactics from Machiavelli's *The Prince*. You can read Don's article, "Influence by Cruelty," at the Mesquite Local News website, **www.mesquitelocalnews.com.** And watch for his forthcoming book on cruelty and other Dirty Tricks. Title: *Vampire Negotiating: How to Suck the Blood Out of The Other Guy.*

Defensive Weapon 4: Remind Big Dogs and Other Guerrillas of Their Competition—Real or Imaginary

Put big dogs and other guerrillas you're dealing with on the defensive. Tell them you have better offers from their competitors, even if you don't. A less powerful version of this is to tell them you can't make a decision until after you contact their competitors. Quite often, people say this just to get rid of the other guy if they have no intention of working with him—it's more polite.

The best times to use this are when the big dog or the other guerrilla starts to play tough, or when it seems likely that the entire deal will end up in an impasse.

Five Winning Guerrilla Counter-Punches

Here are five things you can do when big dogs and other guerrillas try to use this Weapon on you:

- Remember that this is just a *mild* threat. Don't let your ego take control, making your angry and over-react (Preparation 10, *Deal with your ego*).
- Don't say bad things about your competitors (Avoid Dirty Trick 29, *Isolate TOS—use the grapevine to spread rumors about him*). Instead, talk about how good *you* are (Assertive 39, *Act egotistical—I'm the greatest*).
- Just tell them you can't afford to do what they want (Defensive 32, *I have no more money*).

- And don't just tell him—prove it! Show him the numbers (Assertive 104, *Hey, let's look at the record*).
- If nothing else works and if their business isn't too important to you, don't compromise your goals (Preparation 18, *Integrity—never lose it*). Just walk away from the deal (Assertive 68, *Elvis has left the building*).

Defensive Weapon 6: Use Funny Money, Not Real Money

Which one is real money, and which one is funny money?

- Percentages or whole numbers?
- Costs per unit or total costs?

Costs per units and percentages are funny money. Whole numbers and total costs are real money. Why is the difference so important? Let's find out. Here are three examples:

Example One: Seller says: I'll sell this to you for 25 cents a pound. Big dog buyer says: I'll give you 24 cents a pound. What's a lousy penny? Guerrilla seller should do this kind of figuring: There's one million pounds involved in this deal. That means he's asking me to cut my profit margin from $200,000 to $150,000. I'd lose $50,000 if I did that. I'd better tell him 25 cents is my last and final offer.

Example Two: This works even in free-spending Las Vegas. Casinos know that gamblers will make a $100 bet using a $100 chip (funny money) a lot faster than when use a $100 bill (real money).

Example Three: This also works when you're buying a car. Dealers try to get buyers to think only about the monthly payment, not about the total price, including interest payments. They try to give you that information to you only after you've signed the papers—and only if you ask for it.

When the other guy concentrates on funny money instead of real money, you've made him pay attention to the seductiveness of money that doesn't seem entirely real—like a $100 casino chip.

Five Winning Guerrilla Counter-Punches

When the big dog or another guerrilla uses funny money, here are five things you can do:

- Examine the figures in his proposal very carefully (Defensive 22, *Get and verify information*).
- And bring along an expert to help you do this, especially if there's a lot of technical data (Assertive 94, *Intimidate TOS by bringing an expert with you*).
- Go back to the basics of the math you learned in grade school and high school—concepts like average, median, mode, simple annual interest, annual compound interest, and the like. This kind of review will help you (Preparation 2, *Pick your battles carefully—prepare, rehearse, manage your time*).
- Don't be afraid to ask for more time to study their proposal (Defensive 27, *Stall for time—get lost for a while*).
- If his funny money proposal costs you too much in real money, simply tell him, and *don't give in* (Defensive 89).

Defensive Weapon 14: Keep the Other Person's Expectations Low

When you concede, you can almost see the big dog drool. He's expecting even more from you. Here are six ways to keep his expectations low:

- Go slow, even if you really want what the big dog has—and want it badly.
- Make him work hard for each concession you make.
- Don't give up too much too soon to him. Take your time.
- In fact, don't be afraid to take something back if he pushes you too far.
- And instead of making just one large concession, give away a little bit each time. In other words, use Assertive 103—*Nibble away*—in reverse. Many studies say the same thing—the side which makes the biggest dollar concession is almost always the losing side.
- Finally, don't ever tell him "I'll think about it." That's really a concession, and it *always* raises his expectations. Instead, say "What will you give me if I even *decide* to think about it?" That's a really tough give-in (Submissive 12).

Six Winning Guerrilla Counter-Punches

When the big dog actually takes something back he already gave you, you may think the deal-making situation is seriously deteriorating. That's just what he *wants* you to think. What can you do about it?

- *Call his bluff* and ask him why he's doing this (Assertive 51).
- Tell him that taking back a concession he already gave you is a Dirty Trick. This is Assertive 52 (*Ask him "Why are you using Dirty Tricks, and when will you stop"*).
- But if he continually gives you a lot less than what you want, then you've finally got to realize that he's not just trying to lower your expectations. He's not playing games. He's actually playing hardball with you. This is when you should probably stop negotiating and tell him, "*Elvis has left the building.*" (This is Assertive 68.)
- On the other hand, it may be time for you to make a concession if these three *if's* are there:
  - If the big dog really is doing what he wants to do and isn't just bluffing.
  - If your expectations aren't as high as when you began dealing with him.
  - If you *really want* to complete the deal.
- But make sure your concession doesn't mean much to you and means a lot to him (Submissive 1, *Put a dollar value on each concession you and TOS make*).
- Finally, make sure you get something in return from him for what you're doing. Something real, not a promise (Defensive 88, *Use trade-offs, but don't mess with promises*).

Defensive Weapon 29: The Power of Being Unprepared—Forgetting on Purpose

This time, let's see how the big dog tries to use this on you:

Sure, you're powerful when you come into the deal-making session very prepared. But some people get *even more* power by being *un*-prepared, especially if they're less committed to the relationship than the other guy is. It's easy to tell their lack of preparation is just a lie when they use this so-called excuse too often to be believable. For example, they conveniently forget to bring important things with them to the deal-making session—their checkbook, credit card, legal documents, and so forth. And here's what may happen on a larger scale: "Yeah, I know we agreed on a price of $2 million for the real estate, but my partner reminded me that there's an additional $20,000 in loan charges. Sorry about that."

So, whatcha gonna do?

Five Winning Guerrilla Counter-Punches
- Be skeptical (Preparation 7, *Become hard to convince*).
- If your suspicions are correct, then get angry on purpose (Dirty Trick 51, *Scare the hell out of TOS—make him fear you*).
- Don't be afraid to call him a liar (Assertive 51, *Confront TOS—call his bluff*).
- Don't deal with him anymore. Simply walk away (Assertive 68, *Elvis has left the building*).
- And don't bother trying to get *revenge* (Dirty Trick 6) by coming to the negotiating table unprepared the next time yourself—it's just not worth it.

Defensive Weapon 30: Give the Person You're Dealing with the Run-Around

Defensive Weapons 29 and 30 go together. If the big dog often forgets something important, he'll probably also use this avoidance Weapon on you. Here's how he'll do it:

- He's always busy or not there when you call him on the phone or visit him in person.
- He doesn't return your phone calls, doesn't answer your e-mails.
- His secretary tells you he's sick.

His pattern is very easy to spot, especially if he combines avoidance with forgetfulness.

Three Winning Guerrilla Counter-Punches

How long will it take you to get fed up with all this garbage? Here's what we suggest:

- Get angry on purpose (Dirty Trick 51, *Scare the hell out of TOS— make him fear you*).
- Don't be afraid to call him a liar (Assertive 51, *Confront TOS—call his bluff*).
- And don't deal with people who offer other phony excuses over and over, such as "I'm too sick to talk to you today." Just get up, walk away, and never deal with them again (Assertive 68, *Elvis has left the building*).

Defensive Weapon 32: I Can't Afford It—I Have No More Money

This Weapon is simplicity itself. If you want to end the deal-making process, just make a stand and tell the big dog or the other guerrilla, "My well is dry. I have no more assets. Without money, there's no way I can make a deal with you." What you're *really* trying to do here is to lower the cost of the project and bring it down to the level you want. Even if you *do* have the money and are lying to him, your excuse may work because you're temporarily stopping things without taking any blame. It's subtle, and it really works!

Three Winning Guerrilla Counter-Punches

- At the very beginning, find out the size of the big dog's working budget if you can. Two weapons here: Assertive 32 (*Know your enemy and know yourself—knowledge is power*). And Defensive 22 (*Get and verify information*). This will save you the time and trouble of presenting one proposal after another, all of them way beyond his means.
- If his budget is tight, find out if this is temporary or permanent. It it's temporary, try again, perhaps at the beginning of his next fiscal year. The same two Weapons again—Assertive 32 and Defensive 21.
- Use a payback period chart to convince him of the value of your proposal. Make sure it's easy for him to tell that the money he gets is bigger than his costs (Assertive 33, *Be logical—and make sure TOS knows you are*). Your accountants can help you prepare the chart.

Defensive Weapon 42: Don't Give the Big Dog or the Other Guerrilla Very Important Information

There are certain things you don't want anybody to know—ever! For example, how many of you have given your password to the person closest to you in the whole world, your spouse? Probably not many of you. Well, that's obvious. But there are three other important reasons for you to keep your information hidden:

- When it would harm you if the other person had this information.
- When you feel threatened if he learned stuff about you without you learning stuff about him in return. Almost everybody we know seems to have this psychological hang-up.
- When you want to learn how powerful or weak you really are in the eyes of the other guy:
  - You're powerful: If he spends a lot of time trying to get this information from you, this Weapon is working for you.
  - You're weak: If he doesn't seem to care, you're probably not going to get much from him.

Three Winning Guerrilla Counter-Punches

First of all, you've got to be smart enough to know the big dog will never tell you everything you want to know. But if you think he's withholding *important* information from you, here's what you can do:

- Keep probing, keep digging. If you're persistent and aren't too obvious about it, you'll eventually get what you are looking for (Defensive 21, *Appear as harmless as TV's detective Columbo*).
- Act skeptical when he tells you he's given you as much information as he possibly can (Preparation 7, *Become hard to convince*).
- Make friends in his company. They may give you the information you want to know (Defensive 76, *Find allies and use them*).

Defensive Weapon 49: Be Honest—But Only up to the Point Where It Doesn't Hurt You

Nobody ever seems to want to be the first to lay all their cards on the table, so Cooperative Weapon 8 (*Complete honesty—reveal your bottom line*) is very seldom used. Neither you nor the big dog expects this anyway. And too much honesty makes you very vulnerable. So if the big dog uses such words as *frankly* and *honestly*, he's probably over-compensating for the fact that he's really *not* being that honest with you. When we hear those words, we get suspicious. We think you shouldn't use them. And be extra-watchful when the big dog uses them.

The main problem with using this Weapon is that it raises his expectations—he'll expect you to reveal more and more information. This can quickly become a *slippery slope* for you. On the other hand, this is a very powerful Weapon if you use it correctly. Here are four guidelines:

- When you let the big dog know both the pro's and con's of your offer, this subtly tells him you're an honest and trustworthy person. And this means you'll be more persuasive when you tell him about your *genuine* strengths.
- Confess only your *small* weaknesses. If you tell him your *major* weaknesses, you're only screwing yourself. In other words, confessing only your small faults may lead him to think that you have no big faults.
- And don't stop when you tell him your weakness. Follow-up immediately with one of your strong points that's related to your weakness and neutralizes it.
- Finally, convince the big dog or other guerrilla you're being almost totally honest with him by *using your body language* (Defensive 16) and testimonials (Defensive 77, *Find prestigious allies and use them*).

Four Winning Guerrilla Counter-Punches
- Don't just *welcome* the information the big dog gives you—*use* it to win! But be skeptical and test how accurate it is before you act on it (Preparation 7, *Become hard to convince*).
- If he expects you to lay your cards on the table, too, lay only some on the table. And if he's been completely honest with you, lay more of them on the table (Cooperative 4, *Reciprocity*).
- But don't give away all your secrets (Submissive 12, *The tough give-in—bargain harder each time you give up something*).
- Do some digging, and find out what kind of reputation he has (Defensive 22, *Get and verify information*). If most people think

he's fair, be honest with him, too—up to the point where you don't hurt yourself. Remember, you probably didn't give your spouse your password. We didn't either.

Defensive Weapon 71: Constant Nagging—Low-Level Negativity

First of all, we've found that most naggers are guerrillas, not big dogs. Nagging is subtle, and most big dogs aren't comfortable being subtle. We talked about people who make your life miserable in Chapter 11 when we discussed Assertive Weapon 97, *Put TOS on the defensive*. The nagger also makes your life miserable, but he does it in a more subtle way. If you're a sensitive person, this kind of guerrilla may make each encounter miserable for you by finding fault with you, constantly complaining, and being negative in general. He seems to enjoy being picky, demanding, and hard to please. He *nibbles* away by *nagging* away.

Be careful—if he does this often, you're dealing with a bully—the same kind you dealt with in grade school and high school. Watch out for these kinds of people. Don't deal with them. If they think you're weak, they'll pound away at you. They need both victims and oxygen to survive.

Five Winning Guerrilla Counter-Punches

How do you deal with bullies?

It's pretty easy to handle a bully if he works for your company and you have to deal with him regularly:

- First, report him to your supervisor and the right person in the personnel department (Assertive 74, *Tell TOS you're going over his head*). If your company has anti-bullying policies, they might fire him.
- Then, make sure your company *confronts* the bully—as soon as possible (Assertive 52). Make sure they don't delay things, because they'll get worse.
- Cultivate your *grapevine* at work (Defensive 24). People might tell you if he's planning to retaliate against you.
- And protect yourself after work. No telling what he might try to do to you if he wants revenge (Defensive 27, *Get lost*).

And what if the bully works for another company? Stop trying to make a deal with him or people like him (Assertive 68, *Elvis has left the building*). Life's too short. Find somebody else to make a deal with—fast.

Believe it or not, Elvis Presley was bullied a lot when he was a scrawny, shy, teenage nerd in Memphis. He came up with unique ways to avoid bullies. Read Don's article, *Bullying and Elvis Presley*, by going to **www. mesquitelocal news.com**. It was posted on June 4, 2011.

Defensive Weapon 87: You Gotta Do Better Than That!

Directly ask the big dog or the other guerrilla to make you a better offer. But make sure he knows what's in it for him if he gives you a better deal. In other words, support your case by using *reciprocity* (Cooperative 4). Like asking him for a cash discount. Or telling him, "I'll pick up my order. You won't have to deliver it to me. Lower your price by the amount of what it costs to deliver it to me."

And even if you don't support your case, you'll be surprised how many times this works with a sales rep. He'll often lower his price or at least throw in an extra benefit when you ask him, "Is this your best offer?"

Four Winning Guerrilla Counter-Punches
- Don't give big dogs and other guerrillas any information until you're sure what they're really looking for—it's probably more than just a lower price (Defensive 25, *Secure your secrets—adopt a fortress mentality*).
- Even then, remember when you give away information, you're giving the other guy a concession. Never make a concession without getting something in return (Preparation 19, *20 do's and 20 don'ts of making concessions*).
- Say, "This is my best price on this model, but if you don't need this extra feature, I'll sell you this other model for $500 less." This is Defensive 88 (*Use trade-offs, but don't mess with promises*).
- Keep your goal in mind—to win the negotiation. Be firm and don't give in too easily (Submissive 12, *The tough give-in—bargain harder each time you give up something*).

Defensive Weapon 88: Use Trade-Offs, but Don't Mess with Promises

Everybody knows what trade-offs are. But this is a lot more complicated than just getting something in return when you make a concession. What *kind* of something? If anybody—big dogs and guerrillas alike—tries to give you a *promise in return for your concession* (Cooperative 13), tell him this: "I never confuse promises with concessions. You shouldn't either. *Promises are easy to make and hard to keep.* I don't want to raise your expectations to a dangerously high level. So I'm not going to make you a promise, even if I know I can keep it. I'll give you something *real* instead—a concession you can measure in dollars and cents. Please treat me the same way."

Memorize what you just read. Only 68 words! Then try it out. It really works!

Five Winning Guerrilla Counter-Punches

- Always remember—you're under no obligation to make a concession when the guy you're dealing with makes one. There's no pressure at all, so relax and accept your good luck (Preparation 12, *Calm down and lighten up*).
- Try to get the big dog or the other guerrilla to concede first. This gives you a big advantage (Preparation 19, *20 do's and 20 don'ts of making concessions*).
- Don't make one big concession with a large dollar amount. Instead, make several smaller ones (Defensive 14, *Keep TOS's expectations low*).
- If you don't like what he gave up and don't want to give him something in return, say such things as "I'll consider it" and "Let me think about it." This is Defensive Weapon 27 (*Stall for time*). But remember, these words raise his expectations, and the big dog or the other guerrilla might become harder to deal with. So use the words *Let me think about it* with great caution.
- Try to give away *funny money* and get real money in return (Defensive 6).

And after you read Chapter 17, Guerrilla Concession-Making, try out some more of Don's Weapons there.

CHAPTER 13

THREE SUBMISSIVE WEAPONS— POWERFUL AND *OVER*-USED

What this chapter is all about: *Emotion-involving choices, splitting the difference, and accepting defeat.*

Submissive Weapon 3: Drool and Choose— Give Big Dogs and Other Guerrillas Several Choices That Emotionally Involve Them

When you're selling, offer the big dog or the other guerrilla several items and ask him to buy the one he likes best. Better yet, give him a free trial for several of your items. The more time he spends trying out your products and services, the more emotionally committed he is to making a deal with you.

But don't give him too many alternatives. Why not? Because having to differentiate among so many goodies tires him out. When he gets tired, he stops trying, and his motivation to buy goes down. It's true. Here are two findings from a study in the *Journal of Personality and Social Psychology*:

- Only three percent of people bought jam at a supermarket when 24 flavors were displayed. 30 percent bought jam when only six flavors were displayed.

- A lot more people prefer a retirement plan with few options versus a plan many options.

Two Winning Guerrilla Counter-Punches—and One to Avoid
- To keep this relationship going on the right track, *reciprocate*—give him several alternatives as well (Cooperative 4).
- When you're buying, accept the seller's offer with thanks, especially if it's a free trial (Cooperative 24, *Ooze warmth, but try hard to appear sincere about it*).
- But don't act like a greedy kid in a candy store. Don't come back and ask for more and more (Don't use Assertive 103, *Nibble away—wear out the other side—TOS. Outlast him*). He'll think you're a free-loader.

Submissive Weapon 14: Split the Difference
Going 50-50 sounds quite reasonable on the surface. And it often ends a deadlock. However, it's very important for you to remember this: *Whoever says it first is making a big fat dumb mistake. Why? Because that person has the least to lose.* So don't be tempted to say, "Let's split the difference" first. Wait for the big dog or the other guerrilla to suggest it. Then, pounce on him—in a sincere and friendly way, of course!

Chinese merchants in Asia use this often, but not the way most Western deal-makers would use it. After a bit of haggling over price, the merchant takes out two pieces of paper and tells you, "I write my number here. You write your number there. We show each other our numbers. After that, we talk." This is very effective. Try it out. We're pretty sure you'll like what happens.

One Winning Guerrilla Counter-Punch
When he says "Let's split the difference," tell him this: "I can't do it. You have more to gain by going 50-50, and I have more to lose—a lot more. I've never forgotten what I learned in Levinson and Hendon's *Guerrilla Deal-Making* book. They said, 'Whoever says *Let's split the difference* first has the least to lose.' I've got too much to lose if I go 50-50. But to show you what a reasonable person I am, I'll split the difference with you the only fair way—80 for me, 20 for you. I'm sure you know that's the fairest way to do this." Say this with a straight face. Act very, very sincere and friendly—*ooze warmth*, in other words (Cooperative 24).

Submissive Weapon 16: Accept Defeat and Take What You Can Get—Leave Well Enough Alone

It's rare that you get everything you want from the big dog or the other guerrilla. Your ideal solution may be impossible to reach. It's hard to tell, though, when the best thing to do is to take what the other person gives you. Fortunately, you have a rule of thumb. You learned this back in Chapter Six, when we discussed Assertive Weapon 27, *Learn from car dealers—make TOS invest a lot of his time*. If your time is worth less to you than his time is worth to him, don't take what he offers you. Haggle some more. If your time is worth more to you than his is worth to him, accept his offer and take what you can get.

Are you this logical? (Assertive Weapon 33 is called *Be logical—and make sure TOS knows you are*). Most people aren't. They get emotional and throw good money after bad, continually *escalating their commitment* even when they know it's a lost cause (Preparation 13).

Five Winning Guerrilla Counter-Punches

If you still want more, here are five suggestions:

- *Act astonished* when you hear his offer. Let him know you can't believe what a bad deal he's offering you (Assertive 15).
- Try *Hey, let's look at the record*. Support your offer with facts and statistics (Assertive 104).
- Appeal to his *logic* (Assertive Weapon 33) and say "What would you do in my place?"
- Be firm. Stand your ground. This puts pressure on the big dog. Two weapons here: Defensive 89 (*Don't give in to unreasonable demands*). Assertive 66 (*Always keep pressure on TOS*).
- Simply ignore his demands, because both of you know they're unreasonable (Defensive 11, *Don't react at all*).

CHAPTER 14

TWO COOPERATIVE WEAPONS— POWERFUL AND OVER-USED

What this chapter is all about: *Reciprocity and promises.*

Cooperative Weapon 4: Reciprocity— You Scratch My Back, and I'll Scratch Yours

Most of the time, the big dogs and other guerrillas you deal with will want something in return whenever they give you something. If you don't reciprocate, they'll either be disappointed or upset. This puts a lot of pressure on you to give them something, too. But if this creates an obligation that neither one of you want, you'd better not do it.

Subtle Reciprocity

What you just read is somewhat over-simplistic. There's a lot more to reciprocity than just that. Here are three subtle ways to get the guy you're dealing with to give you a lot more than you gave him:

- Make sure he thinks your favor is *significant*.
- If it's *unexpected*, so much the better.

- *Personalize* your requests as much as possible.

This sounds simple, but it's complicated in a subtle way. To show you what we mean, let's look at this example from a scholarly journal:

You're at an upscale restaurant. It gives mints to everybody after they finish their meal. Here are four ways the restaurant can do it. Which one means bigger tips for the waiter?

- Give free mints at the door. You pick them up on your way out. The waiter doesn't give you a free mint when he brings the bill to your table.
- When the waiter presents the bill, he gives one free mint to each person at your table.
- The waiter gives two free mints to each person at your table.
- The Waiter gives one free mint to each person at your table. Leaves. Then comes back, reaches into his pocket, takes out more mints, and gives one more free mint to each person.

Answer: Example One had no effect on the tips the waiter got. Tips went up only three percent in Example Two. Tips went up 14 percent in Example Three. Tips went up 23 percent in Example Four.

Why did this happen? Three reasons:

- *Both unexpected and significant*—two mints seemed significant, one mint is the expected norm.
- *Personalized*—customers think, "Gee I guess the waiter *really* likes me, so I'll give him a bigger tip."

Here's a warning: Don't overuse this Weapon. Why not? People who get gifts and favors become *less grateful* over time. If they receive gifts too often, they start thinking of them as a *right* rather than as your generous gesture. They think: "Don't take away my rights. If you do, I won't cooperate with you anymore." They don't think: "Thanks for your gifts to me over the years. I'm grateful and I'll continue to cooperate." We discussed gratitude vs. rights in Chapter Eight. See Cooperative Weapon 16 there. It's called *The Bonus—Leave something extra on the table at the end.*

(By the way, we talked about *creative* reciprocity in a box in Chapter 11. Sure enough, there's a lot more to reciprocity than just scratching each other's backs.)

Two Winning Guerrilla Counter-Punches

It's dangerous *not* to reciprocate. Everybody—big dogs, other guerrillas, your spouse—expects something in return whenever they give you something. (Your spouse? When she gives you an anniversary present, she appreciates your smiling face.) You certainly don't want to disappoint or anger the person you're dealing with. Not if you want an ongoing relationship with him or her. On the other hand, it's not good to create an obligation that neither of you want. So if you don't want to reciprocate in a meaningful way, try these tactical Weapons:

- Tell the big dog, "I really appreciate what you just did for me. I wish I could give you something in return, but I don't want to exceed the limit my boss imposed on me. I've already reached that limit." This is a combination of two counter-punching Weapons: Defensive 32 (*I can't afford it—I have no more money*) and Dirty Trick 5 (*Limited authority—but first, I have to ask my mommy*).
- Be a good actor. Try and show a little bit of discomfort (but not pain) when you reciprocate, even if you only give him very little (Preparation 19, *20 do's and don'ts of making concessions*).

Cooperative Weapon 13: Make Tempting Promises Instead of Conceding

When you make promises, don't make them just to buy time. That's a bad reason. The big dog will eventually learn you're not sincere. He won't trust you. And this puts your negotiations on a slippery slope—downhill.

Here are six important guidelines. Follow them, and your promises will not only be easy to keep but will make the other person feel good. And your negotiations will stop slipping downward and start moving upward.

- Two kinds of promises work best:
    - Things that are *especially important* to the big dog or other guerrilla.
    - Things you *can actually do.*

- Make promises only if you can keep them. Not keeping them leaves a bad taste in the big dog's mouth.
- You need three things in order to keep your promises:
  - Enough time.
  - Enough authority.
  - Enough resources.
- Put clauses in your contract that let you make adjustments in case certain events take place. Doing this not only lets you to make promises to seal the deal, it but also lets you make changes whenever you have to.
- Promises are over-used in sex. You've got to be imaginative here in order to win the seduction game. Go to **www.GuerrillaDon.com** for unique and powerful flirting techniques. A bonus for you—you'll learn there are many more reasons for engaging in sex—at least 237 reasons. Yes, 237 reasons! This isn't a typo error. And watch for his forthcoming book, *Sex: Get the Honey Without any Money*. Go to his website and send him some of your favorite flirting techniques. They may appear in his book.
- Finally, and most importantly, promises aren't concessions. Concessions can be measured in dollars and cents. Promises are just words. Once again, *that's why they're so easy to make and so hard to keep*! See Defensive Weapon 88. And that's why people use them much more than they use concessions.

Eight Winning Guerrilla Counter-Punches

When the big dog or other guerrilla promises you things, here are four things you can do:

- Don't be naïve and assume he will keep his promises. Maintain a healthy skepticism, especially at the early stages of the deal (Preparation 7, *Become hard to convince*).
- Make sure both of you agree precisely about what you have promised him and what he has promised you. Get all this in writing. Both of you should initial all written promises (Assertive 54, *Control the agreement process itself*).

- Test his promises this way: Get just one promise from him. See if he keeps it. If he does, there's a high probability he'll keep more of his promises (Defensive 22, *Get and verify information—detect and expose bullshit*).
- Watch out for his *tempting promises* (Cooperation 13). Remember, you don't have to give the big dog or the other guerrilla something in return for his promise. Why not? Because a promise isn't a concession.

And suppose you're dealing with him for the first time. He promises you something you want—a lot of future business. But he'll do this only if you do something for him in return—a big discount right away. This happens a lot more often when you're dealing with another guerrilla than when you deal with a big dog. Here are four other things you can do:

- Stay skeptical and don't be tempted to give him a big discount (Preparation 7, *Become hard to convince*).
- Try offering him a small discount instead (Submissive 11, *Contingent offer*).
- Tell him, "I can't do it. It's against our company's policy." This is Defensive 31 (*Be overly bureaucratic*).
- And if he's still persistent, keep him hopeful by telling him, "I've got to check with my boss before I can do this." This is Dirty Trick 5 (*Limited authority—but first, I have to ask my mommy*).

CHAPTER 15

FOUR DIRTY TRICKS—
POWERFUL AND *OVER*-USED

 hat this chapter is all about: Limited authority, scaring by temper tantrums, lying, and the two G-spots—greed and gullibility.

Dirty Trick 5: Limited Authority—
But First, I Have to Ask My Mommy

This is absolutely the worst kind of a *run-around* (Defensive 30). You negotiate in good faith with the big dog or the other guerrilla. Then, when you're ready to sign the deal, he tells you, "I have to OK this with my boss first." Car salesmen almost always do this. They already know your bottom line—all your secrets—and you don't know any of their boss's secrets. Think of it this way: When the sales manager comes in, he's fully clothed, and you're sitting there naked and very vulnerable. You're at a huge disadvantage. He'll always tell you, "Sorry, my salesman exceeded his authority." Then, he'll give you even more bad news: "Sorry my salesman went too far."

Seven Winning Guerrilla Counter-Punches

Here's how to deal with the person who pulls this Dirty Trick on you, not with his boss—three counter-punches:

173

- Know the guy you're dealing with. Find out in advance if he uses this Dirty Trick a lot (Assertive 32, *Know your enemy and know yourself—knowledge is power*). Here's a hint: Guerrillas use this a lot more often than big dogs do. Why? Because big dogs don't want to admit they're not as big as they want you to believe.

- No matter whether you're making a deal with another guerrilla or with a big dog, we advise you to negotiate very, very reluctantly with this kind of person. To find out if he's going to pull this Dirty Trick on you, ask him *very early* in your deal-making process this question: "Do you have the authority to make this deal?" This is Defensive Weapon 22 (*Get and verify information—detect and expose bullshit*).

- If he says he doesn't have the authority and if you want to keep dealing with him instead of his boss, then get his authority limits in writing (Assertive 54, *Control the agreement process itself*).

If you would rather deal with his boss, here are three things you can do:

- Tell him this: "I've got the authority to make the deal. So let me talk to your boss instead of you. This will save us all a lot of time." This is Assertive Weapon 51 (*Confront TOS—call his bluff*). Once again, TOS stands for the other side.

- Don has had good results by saying this instead: "So you don't have the authority to make a deal? Well, here's what I'm going to do. I'm going to bring in one of my subordinates to talk to you. He doesn't have the authority, either. So after you two little boys play with each other for a while, you can bring in your boss, and I'll come back, and we two big boys will make the deal. I don't want to waste my time talking to you anymore." This is Dirty Trick 31 (*Humiliate and ridicule TOS*). It's strange Don has had good results, because this is somewhat *sarcastic* (Assertive 2). Perhaps it works for him because he says it with a smile (Cooperative 24, *Ooze warmth, but try hard to appear sincere about it*). So use this with caution. It's somewhat rude. Do you want to be rude? Or do you want to waste a lot of time and keep getting the run-around?

- If you already know his boss has the final say-so, do this: Get his boss to approve in writing everything you and the subordinate agree on

(Assertive 54, *Control the agreement process itself*). Make sure his boss does it *after each* agreement, not all at once at the end. This is tedious, sure, but it may tire out the subordinate, and he'll want to bring in his boss. This will save a lot of time.

Finally, protect yourself against this Weapon by making a *contingent offer* (Submissive 11). Contingent on what? On approval by *your* boss. This buys time and creates suspense. When you come through with everything you said you would try to do, the subordinate feels good because you've gotten rid of the suspense. Even if you don't come through, the subordinate will give you credit for having tried. Score another point for your side.

Dirty Trick 51: Scare the Hell Out of the Other Guy—Make Him Fear You

If you're *really* angry, sometimes you lose your temper—you yell, scream, swear, and pound your fist on the table. You might tell the big dog or other guerrilla:

- Your offer is an insult.
- What do you think I am—stupid?
- Do you think I'm made of money?

Don't always bite your tongue afterward. There's actually a benefit in doing this: If this happens suddenly and unexpectedly, it may shock the big dog into reality. (We say big dog because guerrillas rarely use this Weapon on other guerrillas.) However, losing your temper is usually counter-productive, because it usually gets him angry, too.

If you're not really angry and use this, make sure you're a good actor. Dirty Trick 55 is *obvious lying*. Make sure you're not obvious. Most people aren't good actors, though. Anyway, use this Dirty Trick as a last resort. But if you use it, make sure you're believable. Remember, F.E.A.R. means *False Evidence Appearing Real*.

If you want to try somewhat gentler ways to show him you're upset, use some of the 18 gestures making up the body language of dominance in Chapter 16.

Finally, whoever uses this Weapon on a regular basis—you or the other person—loses face and doesn't care if he loses face or not. This is the opposite of Cooperative Weapon 17 (*Make sure TOS saves face*). As you learned in Chapter Two, Americans usually don't care much about saving face, so they tend to use anger a lot more than many other nationalities. And so when foreigners deal with Americans, they probably shouldn't bother helping them save face. Americans won't appreciate it and may not even know the foreigner is trying to do this favor for them. Ignorance is bliss.

Three Winning Guerrilla Counter-Punches

- Be brave when the guy you're dealing with loses his temper (*Assertive 70*). Don't let the big dog think he has intimidated you. But don't sit there impassively, either. This means you shouldn't use Defensive Weapon 11 (*No reaction at all*). Let him know he's offended you.
- Don't accept his bullying. Walk out (Assertive 68, *Elvis has left the building*). This is better than escalating things by *threatening him with violence* (Assertive 77), so don't give in to this temptation, even though it feels good to lose your temper in response.
- If you carried a hidden recording device with you to the meeting and you want revenge, call him later and tell him you've just sent the recording to his boss (Dirty Trick 6, *Revenge*). But do this only if it's legal. We know people who have done this, and they tell us that the boss replaced the bully. Then, they made a deal with his replacement.

Dirty Trick 55: Obvious Lying, Not Just Exaggerated Big Talk

Children can spot a lie a mile away. When they do, they often chant, "Liar, liar, your pants are on fire." We all started lying at an early age. And all of us still lie. Sometimes are lies are tiny ones. Sometimes they're white lies, with no serious consequences. Here, we're talking about big, bad, *Dirty* lies that hurt other people.

And, of course, everybody exaggerates, too (Assertive 39, *Act egotistical—I'm the greatest*). Make sure you know the difference between an exaggeration and a lie. Exaggerations have some truth in them and sometimes become *future truths*, but lies are completely false. They just ain't gonna happen!

Here are four other important things you need to know about lying and liars:

- Lies raise other people's expectations. That's bad if you have nothing to back up your big talk. They'll become upset and may walk out.
- Some people, like politicians, are serial liars. They lie so much, they often can't tell the difference between reality and fiction. Serial liars are harder to spot, because when they lie they think they're telling the truth. Their body language indicates honesty. (Watch for Don's book, *Hey, Stupid! How Politicians Lie and Manipulate Voters*. It will be published in 2014. Advance info about it is in **www.GuerrillaDon.com**.)
- Most *normal* liars are easy to spot, though. Why? Because of the way our memories work. Things that *really* happened to us were captured by our five senses. This embeds the events in our memory. Lies didn't happen, they weren't captured by our senses, and they aren't embedded in our memory. We remember things that are embedded in our memory, not things that aren't. So you've got to have a great memory in order to be a good liar. How's *your* memory? Test it by seeing if you can remember the name of Dirty Trick 51.
- Liars need to be good actors. People who know body language find it easy to spot a liar. We'll tell you more about this in Chapter 16.

Five Winning Guerrilla Counter-Punches

- Always be skeptical and extra observant, especially when you're trying to make a deal with somebody new (Preparation 7, *Become hard to convince*).
- *Watch the body language of the big dog or other guerrilla.* It will give you clues as to his honesty or deceitfulness (Defensive 15).
- Whenever you catch him lying, confront him quickly (Assertive 52, *Ask why are you using Dirty Tricks, and when will you stop*). But be careful—you may or not may want him to *feel guilty* (Assertive 80).
- Make friends inside the organization of the person you're dealing with. Use your friends as contacts and information sources. This lets you check their claims and behavior (Defensive 76, *Find allies and use them*).
- If he's threatening to walk out if you don't make a concession, *call his bluff* to see if he's lying or not (Assertive 51). But do this only when the consequences of his telling the truth aren't negative on your side.

Dirty Trick 76: The Two G-Spots: Take Advantage of the Ultimate Loser's Greed and Gullibility

It's easy to get greedy people to trust you if you give them a plausible story, especially one that appeals to their greed. They want to believe they can get something for nothing. And it's also easy to convince gullible people. And so if the other guy is both greedy and gullible, it's going to be a lot easier to get him to do what you want him to do. Bernie Madoff, the con man who stole billions from his investors, didn't work alone. He had many accomplices— his clients. People like him are always looking for greedy and gullible people because they're easy marks. Here's how to tell if somebody's greedy, generous, gullible, or skeptical:

First, how greedy or generous are *you*? If you've led a pampered life, you're probably on the greedy side. On the other hand, people who have been self-reliant for a long time often are more generous. Here are seven other ways to tell:

Greedy	Factor	Generous
None	Number of brothers and sisters	Several
Crowded	Dwelling unit	Uncrowded
More	Cynical	Less
Yes	Self-centered	Not
Less	Cooperative	More
More	Inward-looking—interested in many things that don't affect him	Less
Yes	Selfish	Not

Second, how gullible or skeptical are you? Here are ten ways to tell:

Gullible, High Trust	Factor	Skeptical, Low Trust
Less	Prone to steal and shoplift	More
Less	Prone to cheat	More
A lot more	Number of lies told	A lot less
A lot	Number of friends	Only a few

Less	Inner conflicts	More
More	Happy	Less
Yes	Willing to give other people a second chance	No
Yes	Respect other people	No
A lot	Trust other people	A little
Expects it	Attitude toward consistency in behavior of others	Doesn't expect it
More	Overall adjustment to life	Less

Get to know people in general, not just the person you're trying to make a deal with. Try to figure out if they're gullible and/or greedy. Then, check out the guy on the other side of the negotiating table from you. See if he fits the greedy-gullible pattern. It will be fairly easy to convince him if he's *both* greedy *and* gullible.

Five Winning Guerrilla Counter-Punches

When the big dog or other guerrilla tries to push your greed-gullibility button, here's what you should do:

- Be honest with yourself. Know your assets and liabilities. Two Weapons here: Preparation 10 *(Deal with your ego)* and Assertive 32 *(Know your enemy and know yourself)*.
- If you realize you're greedy and/or gullible, you tend to believe what other people tell you—even stories that seem too good to be true. Be skeptical (Preparation 7, *Become hard to convince*).
- If you get burned, *learn from your mistakes* (Preparation 11).
- In each negotiation, make sure you check to see if the other person is lying to you or not (Defensive 22, *Get and verify information—detect and expose bullshit.*)
- Get his promises in writing, so you can present evidence if you sue him in court for non-compliance (Assertive 54, *Control the agreement process itself*). Don't use Dirty Trick 17—the *frivolous lawsuit*. It's not worth the time or money.

Conclusion and a Look Ahead

Chapters 10-15 covered 50 very powerful and very over-used deal-making Weapons—two Preparation, 27 Assertive, 12 Defensive, three Submissive, two Cooperative, and four Dirty Tricks. In the next major part of your book, you'll learn two things about how guerrillas can win big—by using body language (Chapter 16) and by knowing how to concede (Chapter 17).

PART FIVE

BODY LANGUAGE AND CONCESSION-MAKING FOR GUERRILLAS

Two chapters are in Part Five: Chapter 16 is all about the most powerful Guerrilla Weapon of all—body language. Chapter 17 tells you all about how to make concessions and still win.

CHAPTER 16

GUERRILLA BODY LANGUAGE

What this chapter is all about: Basic training—51 fundamental gestures. Five parts of advanced course—40 lying gestures, 18 dominance gestures, 12 ways to touch, 19 office furniture positions, and manipulating others with your own body language.

Introduction

Your best introduction to this extremely powerful Weapon is to go to *www.YouTube.com* and type in "Donald Hendon." You'll see a 38-minute talk Don made on the essentials of Body Language.

One of the most powerful under-used Weapons is *Know Your Enemy and Know Yourself—Knowledge Is Power* (Assertive 32). You learned all about this in Chapter Six. Guerrillas can learn a lot about big dogs and other guerrillas by watching their body language. You can tell

- Whether they're interested in what you're saying or not. This is Defensive Weapon 15.
- Whether they're lying to you or not. Defensive 15 again.
- Whether they're trying to dominate you or not. Defensive 15 again.

You can also learn a lot about them by observing

- How and when they touch other people, including you. This is Defensive Weapon 18.
- The arrangement of their offices. This is Defensive 19.

And, if you're good at all this, you can use *your own* body language to manipulate big dogs and other guerrillas. This is Defensive Weapon 16.

You'll learn all these things in this chapter. The main thing you'll learn is that body language is all about power. Knowing and using body language gives a guerrilla a lot of power. Don tells his audiences, "Body language is the most powerful and useful skill I have ever learned. Most people don't know body language, even if they think they do. It's a lot more complicated than smiling means good and frowning means bad. And there's a lot more to learn than crossed arms means defensiveness and open arms means open to suggestions. But it's simple to learn. Learning it doesn't mean being skillful at using it, though. To become skilled, you have to practice it a lot." How much is a lot? That depends on you.

This chapter will give you the knowledge you need. Your practice will make you skillful.

How Simple It Really Is

Look at this drawing of a jury in a courtroom. What's going on?

All the men are reacting *extremely* negatively, and all the women *really* like what's going on. The punch line of the cartoon is, "Now tell the jury what you did with the knife, Mrs. Bobbitt." You may remember that in 1993, Lorena Bobbitt cut off her husband's penis with a carving knife after he sexually abused her. She threw it away several miles away from their house. The jury found her not guilty. Sure, the cartoon is funny. But the main thing is that you knew immediately that the two sexes were reacting very differently. The women loved it, and the men were scared.

Catherine Kieu was arrested for doing the same thing in California in July 2011. We hope this isn't the start of a trend.

Here's how simple body language is—there's only six things you need to remember:

The Six Essentials of Body Language

- Watch the big dog or the other guerrilla carefully for about five minutes.
- Don't let him know you're watching him for clues.
- Put each gesture he makes into either a positive or negative category.
- One gesture by itself may not mean anything at all. So look for *clusters* of gestures. They mean a lot.
- If most of his gestures are *positive*, keep doing what you're doing, because he's reacting positively to what you're telling him.
- If most of his gestures are *negative*, change your message immediately, because he's reacting negatively to it

Yes, it's that simple. But you have to know what you're looking for. The rest of this chapter gives you the roadmap. Here's what you'll find in the roadmap:

- Basic Training—the 52 fundamental gestures.
- The five-part Advanced Course.
  - o Body language of lying—40 gestures.
  - o Body language of dominance—18 gestures.
  - o Touch language—12 hints.
  - o Language of office furniture position—19 positions.
  - o How to manipulate the big dog or the other guerrilla with *your own* body language.

Basic Training: Is the Big Dog or Other Guerrilla *Interested* in What You're Saying or Not? Does He *Like* It or Not? The 52 Fundamental Gestures of Guerrilla Body Language

While you're reading this, please remember this chapter fills in the details of Defensive Weapon 15, *Watch the Other Person's Body Language.* We first talked about this Weapon in Chapter Seven.

First, pay attention to the big dog's or other guerrilla's entire body—his face, hands, fingers, arms, legs, back, shoulders, belly, etc. Also where he sits and how close or how far away he is from you. Each gesture tells you what's in his mind—positive, negative, or neutral thoughts.

Pay close attention to these 52 gestures in 22 categories

Entire body
- Positive: Leans forward—interested.
- Negative:
    - Backs away—not interested.
    - Negative: Jerky movements—frustration.

Arms
- Positive: Open, not crossed—open to suggestions.
- Negative: Crossed together—defiant.

Legs
- Positive:
    - Slightly open, not crossed—open to suggestions.
    - Open very wide—sexual gesture.
    - Crossed legs with foot turned toward you—not too negative, sometimes even positive.
- Negative:
    - Crossed legs with his foot turned away from you—very negative, defiant, defensive.
    - Rocking, swinging, tapping—very nervous.
- Neutral: Crossed at ankles—very orderly mind.

Face—Eyes
- Negative:
  - ○ Blinking rapidly—angry, excited, lying.
  - ○ Closes eyes quickly while moving head back at same time—you're too close to him.
  - ○ Nearsighted person takes off glasses—he doesn't want to see you or be seen. (Remember—only if he's nearsighted.)
- Neutral: Intense gaze, whether he's looking at your or not—he's in deep thought, reflection.

Face—Eyebrows
- Negative: Only one eyebrow moves up—he doesn't believe you.
- Neutral: Both eyebrows move up—he's astonished. (Astonishment can be good or bad.)

Face—Chin
- Negative: Chin withdraws into chest—you're too near him, so you should move away.

Face—Overall position
- Positive: Face at an angle, taking lots of notes—very interested.
- Negative:
  - ○ Face at an angle, doodling—very bored.
  - ○ He looks away from you when he begins to speak—he doesn't really want to deal with you.

Face—Movement
- Neutral:
  - ○ Face moves up at end of questions—he's finished, wants you to answer.
  - ○ Face moves down at end of statement—he's finished, wants you to respond.

Fingers—Touching each other
- Positive: Right thumb on top of left—honest.
- Negative: Left thumb on top of right—sneaky.

Steepling and Flying Elbows
- Steepling—fingertips on left hand touching fingertips on right hand, without palms touching—superiority.
- Flying Elbows, an even bigger steepling gesture—putting arms behind head with fingers clenched together and while leaning back. Your boss probably does this when you're at his desk. Extreme superiority.

Thumbs
- Positive: While standing, thumbs in belt, fingers pointing down toward crotch—sexual gesture.

Hands—touching his face
- Positive: Pats hair with one hand—approves of what you're saying.
- Negative: Rubs nose with finger—disapproves of what you're saying.

Hands—touching other objects
- Negative:
    ○ Plays with ring—nervous, anxious, embarrassed.
    ○ Takes ring off finger, puts it into pocket—he's married, wants you to think he's single.

Back
- Positive: Slightly curved—flexible.
- Negative: Very straight, rigid—inflexible, big ego.

Shoulders
- Negative:
    ○ Retracted—angry.
    ○ Raised—afraid.
    ○ Hunched—You're too close to him, so move away.
- Neutral:
    ○ Squared shoulders—carrying out his responsibilities.
    ○ Bowed shoulders—carrying a heavy load.

Belly
- Negative: Over-relaxed—depressed.

Perspires heavily
- Negative: Nervous, tense, especially when it's cool.

Where he sits
- Positive: Diagonally across from you at the corner of your desk—friendly.
- Negative:
  - ○ Directly across from you—antagonistic.
  - ○ At center of table—wants to dominate.
  - ○ Back of room, in corner—he's saying "Leave me alone, I don't want to participate."

Distance from each other, indoors, in U.S.
- 16 to 18 inches: Normal distance for woman-to-woman.
- 18 to 20 inches: Normal distance for man-to-man.
- 22 to 24 inches: Normal distance for man-to-woman. Why further apart? Sexual tension. Ages of the two people make no difference, either.

Distance from each other, indoors, several other nations, including France, Latin America, etc.
- 13 inches, man-to-man is normal.

Distance from each other, indoors, big cities and smaller towns
- People in big cities tend to stand closer together than people from smaller towns.

Distance from each other, on the street
- Positive: When walking on the street, it's OK for him to watch you until you're about eight feet apart. Then he has to turn away.
- Negative: But if he keeps looking at you and you're less than eight feet apart, then he's invading yours space.

Is the Big Dog or Other Guerrilla Lying to You or Not? The Advanced Course in Body Language,

Part One: The Body Language of Lying—40 Gestures

These next 40 gestures are dead giveaways—when the person you're trying to make a deal with makes several of these gestures throughout most of your negotiating session, he's lying to you. Most of them are made because he's nervous about lying to you. Don has found that most of his seminar participants learn the body language of lying a lot faster than body language in general. You probably will, too. Here's what you'll learn about—eyes, fingers, face, hands, hands on the face, feet, shoulders, voice, out-of-synch gestures, and a few miscellaneous gestures.

Eyes
- The big dog or other guerrilla makes almost no eye contact with you. Warning: Experienced liars, like politicians, know that most people think no eye contact means lying. So they often look at you just to make you think they're being honest, even though they're not.

Fingers
- He taps his fingers a lot.

Face
- He blushes, even if it's very faint.
- He licks his lips often.
- He twitches his lips.
- He leaves his mouth slightly open a lot.
- Most prolonged looks that last longer than five seconds are usually lies. An important exception—smiling. It takes 15 facial muscles to smile and 43 facial muscles to frown. So it's easier to smile than to frown. You should watch out for the phony *Jimmy Carter Smile*, which so many politicians often use. Their smiles last a long time. In his seminars, Don pretends he's former president Jimmy Carter and aims a broad, toothy smile at the audience for about 30 seconds. He doesn't say anything. There's lots of laughter and applause. So don't pay much attention to smiles. They can be faked easily. But if the other person is

frowning at you for a long time, he's *really* upset, because he's making a lot of effort to make his frown last for so long. Pay lots of attention to frowns. Not so much attention to smiles.

- The other guy's face is crooked or asymmetrical. Look at the drawings of three faces here. Don uses these three faces in his seminars, too. He asks the audience, "Which face is the liar?" Almost everybody guesses it's face B, and they're right—it's the only face with a crooked, asymmetrical expression. (Face A shows grief. Face C shows apprehension, fear, or even terror.)

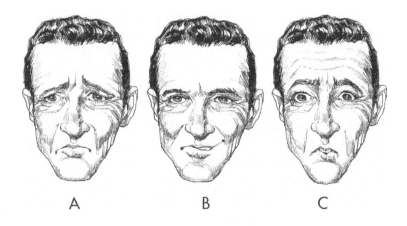

A   B   C

Hands

- The big dog or other guerrilla hides his hands completely. And if he does show his hands to you, he hides his palms. Watch out, though. Very experienced liars know that showing their palms is interpreted as being honest, so they try to convince you they're telling the truth by showing you their palms on purpose.
- He makes much fewer hand gestures.

Hands and Face

- He talks with his hands over his mouth. This is a dead giveaway!
- He briefly touches his nose with his hand. The more often he does this, he more he's lying. Don calls it the *Pinocchio Gesture*. Remember when president Bill Clinton lied about having sex with Monica Lewinsky in his videotaped testimony on August 17, 1998? Two psychiatrists analyzed the 23-minute segment of his testimony when he was lying.

They found he touched his nose *598 times!* That's *26 times a minute!* He didn't touch his nose at all during the two segments of the tape when he was telling the truth. In those two segments, he gave his name, occupation—those kinds of things. And in the same study, the psychiatrists claimed that O. J. Simpson "frequently" touched his nose when he testified about the murder of his wife Nicole and her boyfriend. However, they didn't define "frequently." They published their results in a scholarly journal.

- He tugs at his earlobes, sometimes even yanking them hard.

Feet
- While he crosses his legs, he waves his foot in a circular direction.

Shoulders
- He briefly lifts just one shoulder. Very, very slightly. Quite often, it's hard to see this involuntary gesture. Don's *YouTube* video shows this gesture.

Voice
- The pitch of his voice goes up slightly.
- He makes more speech errors.
- He rambles excessively without coming to the point.
- He stammers more often.
- He clears his throat just before saying something.
- He makes an obviously phony cough just before he says something. Watch out here, though. There could be other meanings—doubt or surprise.
- He makes an obviously phony laugh.
- He whistles.

Out-of-Synch Gestures
- If the other person's mouth is smiling, his eyes should be smiling, too. If not, he's lying. This is hard to spot. Or is it? Here's a reproduction of part of an ad showing an airline stewardess' face. The copy reads, "Cover her mouth with your hand and see what happens to your

friendly hostess (from a rival airline)." Go ahead and do it. What do you see? The eyes of a demon, with a phony smile.

- If his body and face isn't in synch, he's lying. For example, if he bangs the table to indicate he's angry with you without showing an angry face, he's lying. This is even easier to detect if he bangs the table and then puts on his angry face a split-second later.
- His voice and body movements should be in synch. If he says "Yes" while moving his head slowly from left to right and back again several times, he's lying. Why? Because when a person moves his head up and down, he's telling you "Yes." When a person moves his head sideways, he's telling you "No." (In all cultures except for some parts of India.) People who lie for a living—politicians—take this one step further. They not only move their head from left to right and back when saying "Yes," they also move their *entire bodies* from left to right and back. Tape a politician on the podium sometimes. Then fast-forward it. It's a lot easier to notice the left-right-left-right movement that way.

Four Other Gestures
- The big dog or other guerrilla fidgets a lot. That is, he puts his finger inside his shirt collar and moves it around. He also plays with his collar. He adjusts his clothes—tie, coat, pants. Women sometimes adjust their skirts and bras.
- He plays with his ring, keys, and other personal objects.

- While standing, he shifts his weight from foot to foot a lot.
- He paces back and forth.

Two final things to be aware of:

First, it's amazing how easy it is for Don's seminar participants to learn the body language of lying so quickly. Right after he finishes talking about it, he puts them into groups of two. They stand up and face each other. Then, they tell each other their real birthday and a phony birthday. Most of the time, members of his audience are able to tell which birthday is real and which one isn't. Try it yourself with somebody else who has read this chapter of your book.

Second, it's harder to tell if experienced liars, such as car dealers and politicians, are lying, because they lie for a living. They know which gestures mean lies and so they try hard not to make those gestures. When you're dealing with these kinds of people, watch their faces for micro-movements. This is much too complicated a subject to talk about here. To learn more about micro-gestures, go to **www.GuerrillaDon.com**.

Part Two of Advanced Course: Is He Trying to Dominate You? The Body Language of Dominance—18 Gestures

Part Two gives you details about Defensive Weapon 16, which we covered briefly in Chapter Seven.

Here's how to tell if the big guy or other guerrilla is trying to dominate you. Look for these 18 manipulative gestures:

Eyes
- He stares long and hard at you.
- Or, he completely ignores your face when he talks to you.

Face
- He looks bored.
- He frowns.
- He snarls.
- He sneers.
- He smirks.
- He doesn't smile very often—he's overly serious.

Shaking hands

- He has an extra-strong squeeze when he shakes your hand. He interprets a limp handshake as a sign of weakness, so make sure your handshake is as strong as his is.
- If he uses both his hands, he either considers you a very close friend or is trying to put you off-guard so he can dominate you later.
- He keeps his hand on your hand longer than usual.
- He shakes hands with his palm facing downward, not upward. That shows he's on top, you're on the bottom.

Height

- He intentionally stands or sits in an area that's higher than the area you're in—this makes him appear taller, and this gives him an advantage.
- He wears elevator shoes. She wears high heels. Again, this makes them appear taller.

Size

- He stands with his hands on his hips. His elbows stick out. And his legs are apart. All this makes him appear bigger than you.

Space

- He invades your territorial space. Earlier in this chapter, you learned this about territorial space: In most Western cultures, two men usually stand 18 inches apart, two women stand 16 inches apart, and a man and woman stand 22 to 24 inches apart. You also learned that if you're passing somebody on the street, you can look at him until you're about eight feet apart. If you keep looking at him when you're closer, you're invading his space.

Status symbols

- He intentionally displays as many status symbols as he can. Examples: A trophy wife or trophy husband. An expensive Rolex watch. A Louis Vuitton handbag. A large color photo of him and the President on the wall behind his desk, personally signed by the President Big dogs do this a lot more than guerrillas.

- Sometimes, he doesn't intentionally display status symbols. Instead, he subtly displays his power. We gave you six ways this is done when we discussed Assertive Weapon 41, *Imply your power—don't intentionally display it.* See Chapter Six.

Part Three of Advanced Course: The Body Language of Touching—12 Hints to Follow

Touching (Defensive Weapon 18) is the most intimate part of body language. Be cautious when you touch the big dog or the other guerrilla. And be careful how you react when he touches you. Here are 12 things to be aware of:

- Touching the person you're dealing with can help you close the sale. For example, Mary Kay Cosmetics sales reps are trained to touch potential buyers while complimenting them on how good they look when they use Mary Kay products.
- Women touch each other more often than men touch other men.
- People of the same age touch each other more often than do people whose ages are quite different.
- If you think the other person wants sympathy from you, touch him. He or she will like it.
- But be careful. We often touch other people to interrupt them. When you do, touch only the arm or shoulder. And remember, a lot of people don't like you to touch them at all.
- Never touch the other person's private parts unless you're having sex with him or her.
- Who touches other people the most? Younger and older people do. People whose ages are in the middle don't touch others as much.
- Friends touch each other more than strangers do. So before touching them, ask yourself, "Is he a friend, a mere acquaintance, or a stranger?"
- Touching is used for both domination and friendship. When you *poke* somebody, you're usually trying to dominate him. Friendship touching is softer.

- In the Middle East and some Asian nations, especially Thailand, you'll often see two men holding hands. Don't interpret this as a sexual gesture. It's the norm.
- Thais, Koreans, and certain other Asian nationalities touch members of the same sex on the arms often. This is an expression of comradeship, not homosexuality.
- However, in Western nations, touching the other person is almost always perceived as an invasion of space. That can be dangerous.

Part Four of Advanced Course: The Language of Office Furniture Placement—19 Positions

One picture is worth a thousand words. Here are four drawings and 19 questions.

Look at this drawing of the big dog's office. Assume you're invited there to discuss a deal. Answer these questions:

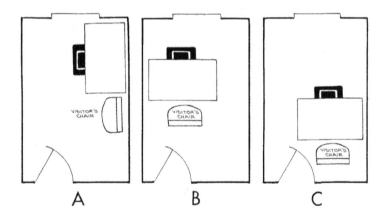

Question: Which office layout gives the big dog the most power? A, B, or C? Why?

Answer: C. He has the most space. He's squeezing you into the smallest space. He's least powerful in layout A.

Here's another drawing:

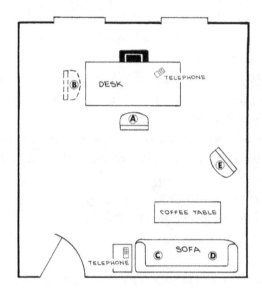

- If the big dog is serious about business, where would he ask you to sit? A, B, C, D, or E?
- Answer: A. Facing his desk.
- If he is being friendly, where would he ask you to sit?
- Answer: He would move chair A to position B.
- If he wants to delay things, where would he ask you to sit? And where would he sit?
- Answer: You at D, on the sofa. He at C, next to his phone.
- If he wants to smooth things over with you, where would he ask you to sit? Where would he sit?
- Answer: He would ask you to sit at D, on the sofa. Again, he would sit at C, next to his phone.
- If you're an aggressive visitor, where would you sit?
- Answer: You move the chair yourself from A to B. Or you sit at C (on sofa), cutting the big dog off from his phone.
- What's the weakest position, for either the big dog or you?

Answer: E

Next, suppose you're at a meeting with several people. Look at the round table in the meeting room. The numbers refer to a clock.

- What's the most powerful position?
  Answer: 12 o'clock
- What's the second most powerful?
  Answer: One o'clock
- What's the least powerful?
  Answer: 11 o'clock

Finally, suppose you're at a meeting with the manager and six other people. Here's the table:

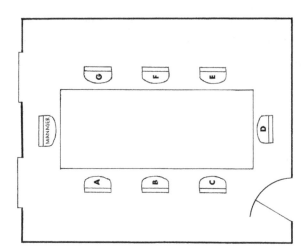

The manager occupies the most powerful position. Where are the best locations?

- For a strong subordinate?
  Answer: F
- For a weak subordinate?
  Answer: E
- For presenting a new idea?
  Answer: B
- For giving a routine report?
  Answer: A
- For a newcomer?
  Answer: G
- For starting a fight?
  Answer: C
- For an outside observer?
  Answer: D

Part Five of Advanced Course: How to Manipulate Others with Your Own Body Language

You always want big dogs and other guerrillas to agree with you. It's actually easier than you think to actually manipulate them into agreement (Defensive 16). But you probably don't think so right now. We think it's important for you to know why this Weapon works so well. Have you heard the term *social contagion*? How about *likes attract*? What these terms mean is that people mimic each other. A lot more than you think they do. Google the *Framingham Heart Study*. You'll find a series of articles on the subject of social contagion by a couple of professors at Harvard and University of California at San Diego. These articles tell you that close friends influence you a lot more than you think they do: If they're fat, you're likely to be fat, too. If you smoke, ditto. If you stop smoking, ditto. The same thing for drinking, loneliness, divorce, happiness, and unhappiness. Your relatives and neighbors don't influence you nearly as much as your friends do.

This topic gets even more interesting—even strange. Here are a few findings from scholarly journals on the subject:

- Participants were given a survey to fill out. Thirty percent of them returned it to a person with a name that didn't sound like their own. 56 percent returned it to a person with a name that sounded like their own. (Don Hendon and Ron Herndon, for example.) This means that your clients may be more receptive to a sales pitch from you if you are similar to them in such things as hometowns, alma maters, birthdays, beliefs, and sex. So talk about your similarities before you make a sales pitch. Examples: "Hey, we both went to the University of Texas at Austin. When were you there?" And "So you're from Mesquite, Nevada. I'm from Mesquite, Texas. How about that!"
- Many people are attracted to professions with names similar to their own (Dennis becomes a dentist, but not a menace). Quite often, people marry others with a similar-sounding first or last name (Charles and Charlotte, Jay and Jeannie, Don and Donna).
- Many people prefer products whose first letter matched the first letters of their own name. (Sam chooses Snickers. Alan chooses Almond Joy. Jay Levinson does, too. He also likes Life Savers. Don Hendon chooses Dove Bars and Hershey Bars. But not at the same time.)

Skeptical? Can you actually use any of this to get the big dog to do what you want him to do? Try this: When you're designing a proposal, put words in the title that reminds him of himself—or even just the first letter of his name. See what happens.

If you're still not sure if manipulating the big dog with your body language is going to work, here's an exercise Don gives his seminar participants at the end of his body language seminars. Try it, and you'll see how well you it works.

Don starts out by giving these instructions:

- Get into groups of two. One of you is the buyer, the other one is the seller. Decide now which is which. Buyers raise your hands. Now, sellers raise your hands.
- This exercise lasts for 20 seconds only.
- Nobody speaks to each other. Just look at each other and give each other some of the body language gestures you've just learned.

- You buyers give the sellers all the negative body language gestures you can think of during the entire 20 seconds.
- You sellers, do this: For the first ten seconds, give the buyers all the *negative* body language gestures you can think of. Then, I'll clap my hand and say "Positive." Sellers then give the buyers all the *positive* body language gestures you can think of. During the entire 20 seconds, you buyers stay negative.
- What's the purpose of all this? I want to see what's going on in the buyer's mind when the seller gives him *negative* gestures, and what's going on in the buyer's mind when the seller gives him *positive* gestures.
- Any questions?
- If no questions, begin right now.

After the 20 seconds have passed, Don asks the participants, "What went on in the buyer's mind when the seller was being negative?" They always answer, "Even more negativity."

Then, Don asks them, "What went on in the buyer's mind when the seller was being positive?" They always answer, "It was hard to stay negative. We became a lot more positive, in spite of ourselves."

This *always* happens: Things get worse during the first ten seconds when both sides are giving each other negative gestures. During the second ten seconds, buyers find it hard to stay negative. They smile, become positive, often laugh self-consciously.

But Wait, There's More…Very Advanced Stuff

Body language isn't just about gestures. In this chapter, we've also talked about voice, position, touch, invading space, height, and even perspiration. Don covers other topics in his body language seminar, including these:

- Micro-movements of the face which gives other card players information about what kind of hand you have.
- Bluffing and calling the other person's bluff.
- Power symbols.

- Power colors, including the most powerful color combinations. Examples: Why blue seems to be the most powerful color, why red is frightening.
- Power clothes.
- Private bathrooms.
- The foot.
- Yellow paper pads.
- Feng shui.
- Flirting and seduction.
- How to pick a jury.
- Body language in job interviews.
- What robbers look for in a victim—how *muggable* are you, in other words.
- How customs and security officials at the airport pick people to search more thoroughly.
- What you can do if the other person's an expert in body language.
- Body language differences in other nations.
- Sending wrong signals and what to do about it.
- Even handwriting analysis. Here are the basics: Upward slant shows optimism, downward pessimism. Overly fancy signature, almost a drawing: Superiority, narcissistic.

If you are unable to attend Don's one-day Body Language seminar, you can learn more about these topics by going to **www.GuerrillaDon.com**. And look for his forthcoming book, *Guerrilla Body Language*.

Conclusion

As we said at the beginning of this important chapter, *Body Language* is the most powerful skill Don has ever learned in his life. It's turned him into a winner. Master it, and you'll win even more than you ever did before!

Now, let's look at how to make concessions and still win big.

CHAPTER 17

GUERRILLA CONCESSION-MAKING

What this chapter is all about: *Seven concession patterns, dollar value of a concession, 20 do's, and 20 don'ts.*

Concessions are *always* on the minds of deal-makers. Neither the big dog nor the guerrilla really wants to make them, but both sides know they're necessary. It's sort of a love-hate relationship. This chapter gives you the most important things you'll need to know about how to use guerrilla Weapons that will turn your concessions into big wins for you.

Part One is about recognizing concession patterns, both yours and the big dog's. It fills in the details of Defensive Weapon 20.

Part Two shows you an easy way to put a dollar value on each and every concession. It's all about Submission Weapon 1.

And Part Three gives you 20 do's and 20 don'ts—Preparation Weapon 19. Follow these 40 important guidelines when you're making concessions to the guy on the other side of the table, whether he's a big dog or another guerrilla.

Part One: How to Recognize the Concession Patterns You and the Big Dog or the Other Guerrilla Make

Chapter Six is where you first read about *under*-used Defensive Weapon 20, *Observe and Record the Concession Patterns You and the Other Person Make*. Now let's *really* learn how to make concessions by looking at the next box:

Don Hendon's Concession-Making Exercise

Copyright (c) 2001-2012 by Dr. Donald Wayne Hendon

Please assume the following things:

- You and the big dog or another guerrilla meet to make a deal.
- You've allocated one hour, 11 a.m. to 12 noon to the negotiating session
- But you don't know how much time he is going to stay at the table with you.
- And you haven't told him your 12 noon deadline either.
- To keep it simple, assume he'll make $100 worth of concessions to you during that hour. That's the limit his boss gave him. His boss also told him to give away the entire $100.

Here are seven ways the big dog or other guerrilla can give you the $100. As you study these seven patterns, what can you conclude from each one? Pay attention to the *amount* of each concession and *when* each one is made.

Give-away Pattern	11:15 a.m.	11:30 a.m.	11:45 a.m.	12:00 noon
1	$25	$25	$25	$25
2	$50	$50	Zero	Zero
3	Zero	Zero	Zero	$100
4	$100	Zero	Zero	Zero
5	$10	$20	$30	$40
6	$40	$30	$20	$10
7	$40	$35	$30	Uh-oh, I've got to take $5 back or my boss will fire me for exceeding my limit

To keep things simple, forget about the obvious—what the other guy concedes depends on what *you* concede. And vice-versa. And, of course, the timing of concessions depends on the situation. Be that as it may, what can you conclude from these seven different concession patterns, no matter who makes them—you or the other person?

If you've already written down your conclusions when you read Chapter Six, refer to them. If not, go ahead and do the exercise now. And if you're going to negotiate as a team, here's a good suggestion: Gather all the members of your team together and work on this jointly. You'll get more insight by doing it as a team, so we recommend this instead of doing it by yourself.

Finished? If so, read on—here's what the seven patterns mean:

Pattern One: 25, 25, 25, 25. Very bad. You consistently give away $25 each time. You're just too darn predictable. The other team's probably keeping score. They'll think, "Wow, this is like playing a broken slot machine at a Vegas casino. All I've got to do is keep saying *no* each time, and I'll get another $25." (Or $250, or $2,500, whatever the amount actually is.) So we don't like this pattern at all. Don't use it.

Pattern Four: 100, 0, 0, 0. Just as bad. Most people—including us—hate this pattern. You're laying your cards on the table too early. You've revealed your bottom line at the beginning, and so you have no more flexibility during the rest of the deal-making process. This is a good pattern to use *only* if you and the other person have been negotiating for a long time. You say: "Here's my bottom line." He says: "Here's my bottom line." Then you both say at the same time, "OK, we're finished, so let's celebrate by going to lunch."

Pattern Two: 50, 50, 0, 0. This is similar to Pattern Four—lots of generosity at first, then nothing at the end. Most people, guerrillas and big dogs alike, don't like to use this pattern very much, either. Neither do we. But when you *do* use it, you're telling the other side you're trying to be honest and up-front early, and this is good—maybe. It's not good if you're dealing with an evil opponent who only wants to take advantage of you.

Pattern Three: 0, 0, 0, 100. We think this is too darn hard-nosed. You should give away something earlier to get some momentum going. However, many people like to use it—especially those in certain nations. We'll tell you which ones shortly.

Pattern Five: 10, 20, 30, 40. An escalating pattern. This is the pattern we dislike the most. The other team is probably keeping score of your concession pattern. They don't know you have only $100 to give away. They don't know the negotiation's going to be over at 12 noon, either. They'll take $10, then $20, then $30, then $40. They'll expect $50 next time, then $60, then $70.

Pattern Six: 40, 30, 20, 10. This is our favorite pattern. It tells the other guy, "My well's getting drier and drier all the time."

Pattern Seven: 40, 35, 30, take 5 back. Many people, especially Asians, really dislike this pattern. Asians don't like it because they feel they'll lose face if they take $5 back. But people in most western nations think "Anything goes until I sign the final contract." We sort of like the pattern because, once again, you're telling the other guy, "My well's getting drier and drier all the time—my boss will fire me if I screw up." On top of that, it sends him an even stronger message than pattern six sends.

Since Don has given seminars in 36 nations on 6 continents to more than 60 nationalities, he has a very large database of tens of thousands of people who like and dislike these seven patterns. Here are some of the things Don has found:

Pattern Three, the overly tough one: The number one choice of Americans, Brazilians, Germans, and South Africans. Watch out when you negotiate with these four nationalities, because you're going to be dealing with hard-nosed people.

Pattern Five, the escalating one: The number one choice of people in Uruguay, Brazil, Kenya, Papua New Guinea, the Philippines, Malaysia, and Singapore. Warning: Don't think everybody in these nations are poor negotiators. Many of them are very, very good. By the way, this is the second favorite pattern of American negotiators, too.

Pattern 6, the de-escalating one: The number one choice of the best negotiators we've ever seen—people from Taiwan, Australia, and New Zealand. They'll eat you up and spit you out! People in Canada, the U.K., Germany, Finland, Chile, Colombia, Peru, and Thailand also liked Pattern 6, but not as nearly as much as did people from Taiwan, Australia, and New Zealand.

Patterns One, Two, Four, and Seven: Almost nobody picked these three patterns. They are mostly unused. If you use them, you'll surprise whoever you're dealing with, the big dog or another guerrilla. Before you decide to use them, though, ask yourself if it's going to be a good surprise or a bad surprise.

Disliked patterns: People in most nations agreed more about what they did *not* like. Almost everybody disliked pattern four, where you gave away

$100 at the very beginning. And almost every nation's second pick for worst pattern was number seven, where you take $5 back.

For in-depth information about how executives in these and many other nations make concessions, please go to **www.GuerrillaDon.com**, The data is taken from Don's database of thousands of executives. You can get reports for specific nations there.

Both Don and Jay hope this discussion of patterns has shown you how important it is to *keep careful records of the concessions* both you and the person on the other side make (Defensive 20). There's usually an underlying pattern. Knowing this pattern will help you get what you want from him, whether he's a big dog or another guerrilla—and probably a lot more, too.

Part Two: How to Put a Dollar Value on Each Concession You and the Big Dog or the Other Guerrilla Make

Accountants are good at putting dollar values on everything. If you're not an accountant, get the help of accountants in your company. They'll need data from you, though. Here's a quick exercise Don's used in his seminars to help you and your accountants figure out if the thing you're negotiating about should be priced high or low:

Putting a Dollar Value on Your Concessions: Exercise

Copyright (c) 2001-2011 by Dr. Donald Wayne Hendon

Look at these 16 pricing criteria:

High price	Pricing criteria	Low price
	1. Change—rate of technological change	
	2. Distribution channels—length	
	3. Inventory turnover	
	4. Manufacturing process—type	
	5. Market coverage	
	6. Market share	
	7. Product life cycle	
	8. Production inputs	
	9. Product—lifetime of product usage	

	10, Product—planned obsolescence	
	11. Product—type	
	12. Product—versatility	
	13. Promotion—contribution to success of product line	
	14. Promotion—dollar amount required	
	15. Return on investment—payout length	
	16. Services—amount of extra's offered	

Now, get together a team from your Accounting, Finance and Marketing departments. Look at these 16 groups of polar-opposite adjectives. The two words in each group are in alphabetical order—for example, the adjectives in both Groups One and Three are *fast* and *slow*. Decide what adjective should be placed under *high price* and what adjective should be placed under *low price* in the box above.

1. Fast. Slow.
2. Long. Short.
3. Fast. Slow.
4. Custom-made. Mass-produced.
5. Intensive. Selective
6. Large. Small.
7. Earlier. Maturity stage.
8. Capital-intensive. Labor-intensive.
9. Long. Short.
10. Long-lived product. Short-lived product.
11. Commodity product (all brands are similar). Proprietary product (valuable brand name).
12. Multiple-use. Single-use.
13. Little. Much.
14. Little. Much.
15. Long-term. Short-term.
16. Few or none. Many.

Don't look at the answers until *after* you've done this exercise. Here they are:

High price	Pricing criteria	Low price
Fast	1. Change—rate of technological change	Slow
Long	2. Distribution channels—length	Short
Slow	3. Inventory turnover	Fast
Custom-made	4. Manufacturing process—type	Mass-produced
Selective	5. Market coverage	Intensive
Small	6. Market share	Large
Earlier	7. Product life cycle—stage	Maturity stage
Labor-intensive	8. Production inputs	Capital-intensive
Long	9. Product—lifetime of product usage	Short
Short-lived product	10. Product—planned obsolescence	Long-lived product
Proprietary (valuable brand name)	11. Product—type	Commodity (all brands are similar
Multiple-use	12. Product—versatility	Single-use
Little	13. Promotion—contribution to success of product line	Much
Much	14. Promotion—dollar amount required	Little
Short-term	15. Return on investment—payout length	Long-term
Many	16. Services—amount of extra's	Few or none

Feedback given to Don from his clients indicates this is an exceptionally valuable tool. Guerrillas especially feel this way. Use this Weapon—Submissive 1—and prosper.

Part Three: How You Can Make Concessions the Right Way: 20 Do's and 20 Don'ts. All of Them Have to Do with Keeping the Expectations of the Big Dog or the Other Guerrilla as Low As Possible

Here's how to put it all together. Follow Don's guidelines, and you're on your way to becoming a big winner.

20 Do's:

Acting:

1. Make the big dog or the other guerrilla think your concession is valuable to you when it isn't. Be a good actor. *(Dirty Trick 55, Obvious lying, not just exaggerated big talk)*

2. *Show physical pain on your face* whenever you make a concession. Make him think your concession hurts you. *(Assertive 16)*

Agents:

3. Use an agent to negotiate for you instead of directly negotiating with the big dog or other guerrilla. Agents usually make fewer concessions, and their concessions are usually smaller. *(Assertive 37, Use a professional or agent to assist you)*

Attitude:

4. Always remember: If you're willing to *settle* for less, you'll usually *get* less. A mild degree of greed is good. *(Dirty Trick 76, The 2 G-spots: Take advantage of the ultimate loser's greed and gullibility)*

Deadlines:

5. Set a deadline only if you want to use it as an ultimatum. *(Assertive 28, Use deadlines wisely)*

6. Try to find out the big dog's deadline. To see if he's serious about it, test him to see if he'll change his deadline. If it's negotiable, it's not a valid deadline. Big hint: Most deadlines are negotiable. *(Defensive 22, Get and verify information—detect and expose bullshit)*

Dollar value:

7. *Put a dollar value on each concession you make.* Tell both the big dog and other guerrilla how much this concession is costing you, if it's to your advantage. *(Submissive 1)*

8. Try to estimate the dollar value of each concession he makes, too. This means you need to find out his cost information, and this may be hard. *(Defensive 22, Get and verify information)*

9. Concede with *funny money* instead of real money—percentages, price per unit. As you learned in Chapter 12 when we discussed Defensive Weapon 6, percentages sound smaller than dollars. $1 per unit sounds low, but if you're buying a million units, that's a million dollars you're going to spend. Getting him to lower his price by two cents per unit will save you $20,000. That's worth haggling about. *(Defensive 6)*

10. Break big concessions into several small ones. Give them away over time. The minds of both big dogs and guerrillas work this way: Several smaller concessions seem much larger than one big one, even if the total dollar amount is the same. *(Assertive 105, 106, and 107: Foot-in-the-door--barely; wiggle your toes; kick door down)*

11. Give yourself a lot of room. If you're selling, start high. If you're buying, start low. *(Assertive 48, Size matters—the big pot)*

12. Keep careful records, but don't let the guy you're dealing with know you're doing this. See if he has a pattern—escalating, de-escalating, waiting until the end. This makes it easier to predict what he's going to do. *(Defensive 20, Carefully observe and keep records of concession patterns—yours and the other person's)*

13. Make both big dogs and guerrillas work hard for everything they get from you. They'll appreciate your concession more. And they'll think they're worth more, too. But if they get your concession too easily, too quickly, they won't think it's that valuable. *(Submissive 10, One step at a time)*

14. Always ask yourself, "Is my concession a reasonable one?" If it's not, don't make it. *(Assertive 33, Be logical—and make sure TOS knows you are)*

Limited authority:

15. Use it. Say "I have to check with my boss before I can give you that concession." *(Dirty Trick 5, Limited authority—but first, I have to ask my mommy)*

Listen well:

16. Listening to what the big dog or other guerrilla says is the cheapest concession you can make—and the most important one to you. *(Cooperative 14, The cheapest concession of all—listen, and listen well)*

17. Listen well, this time with your eyes: *Watch his body language* when he concedes to find out if his concession is important to him or not. *(Defensive 15)*

Timing:

18. Make concessions slowly. Space them out. *(Assertive 26, Extend negotiations over long periods of time)*

19. If you concede first, make sure it's only a minor concession. *(Preparation 22, Gain momentum by making first offer yourself)*

Trade-offs:

20. Always get something in return from the big dog or other guerrilla when you make a concession. But don't accept his promise. *(Defensive 88, Use trade-offs, but don't mess with promises)*

20 Don'ts

Assumptions:

1. Don't assume *reciprocity* is always necessary after each concession. There's got to be an end sometime. *(Cooperative 4—don't carry it to the extreme)*

2. Don't assume that when you give in on one issue, you'll automatically give in on another issue. You're not necessarily on a slippery slope. When you're on a sticky slope, the ground ahead of you isn't endangered by your concessions. The trick is to create meaningful sticking points with your concessions. "Think sticky, not slippery." *(Submission 12, The tough give-in—bargain harder each time you give up something)*

Deadlines:

3. Never tell anybody what your deadline is. It's more dangerous when another guerrilla knows your deadline, but don't let the big dog know it, either. When you tell anybody what your deadline is, you're giving away a lot of your power. That's a dumb concession to make. Once the other guy knows your deadline, he'll probably keep stalling for time, and he will seriously negotiate only when your deadline is almost there. You'll make a lot more concessions then, because you're under a lot of time pressure. *(Assertive 28, Use deadlines wisely. And Assertive 32, Know your enemy and know yourself—knowledge is power)*

4. Don't forget the 80-20 rule: 80 percent of all serious action happens in the last 20 percent of the time before the deadline, whether it's your deadline or the big dog's deadline. *(Preparation 3, Avoid paralysis of perfection—set priorities. Use the 80-20 rule)*

5. Flexibility: Don't set a deadline yourself. Deadlines limit your flexibility. So don't worry about them too much. Always ask yourself, "Whose deadline causes me the most trouble? His or mine?" *(Preparation 5, The right attitude—I've got to earn the right to learn TOS's needs)*

6. Worries: Don't worry about his deadline, either. Always remember, the deadline of both the big dog and another guerrilla limits *their* flexibility, not *yours*. So let the other guy worry about it. *He* has to defend it. You're a lot more flexible without a deadline. *(Preparation 12, Calm down and lighten up)*

Dollars:

7. Never make the largest single concession in the deal-making process. We mean *never!* The person who does this almost always wins a lot less than the other person does. So don't be a loser—make only small concessions. *(Assertive 103, Nibble away—wear out TOS, outlast him—but in reverse)*

Ego:

8. Don't walk out when the big dog or another guerrilla makes you a ridiculous offer. Control your ego. Be polite. See where he's going with this ridiculous offer. *(Preparation 10, Deal with your ego)*

9. Don't insult him when he makes you a ridiculous offer. *(Don't use Dirty Trick 31, Humiliate and ridicule TOS. Don't use Dirty Trick 51 either—Scare the hell out of TOS—make him fear you)*

10. Don't want to be liked so much that you'll *give away the store just to see the other guy smile.* Like yourself so much that you don't care if he likes you personally or not—*deal with your ego. (Preparation 8—Give away store. And Preparation 10—Ego)*

Mistakes:

11. Don't hide your mistakes. Telling the big dog you made a mistake when you take back your concession makes it easier for him to accept what you did. *(Defensive 85, Admit your mistakes and apologize before TOS tries to blame you)*

12. Don't make *too many* mistakes, though. Both big dogs and other guerrillas will think you're pretty dumb—or you're trying to make a fool out of them. *(Preparation 11, Mistakes—admit them, learn from them)*

Timing:

13. Don't make the first concession. Keep your demands hidden while he reveals his to you. *(Assertive 23, When to speak, when to pause)*

14. Don't be afraid to take a concession back, either. Anything goes until both you and the big dog sign the final contract. *(Assertive 54, Control the agreement process itself)*

15. Don't *ever* be the first one to say "Let's split the difference." This is probably the biggest *don't* of all. Why? This tells the person you're dealing with what your bottom line is before you know his bottom line. The person who says "Let's split the difference" first has the *least* to lose. *(Don't use Submissive 14, Split the difference)*

16. Don't make a single concession without knowing *all* of his demands first. *(Assertive 32, Know your enemy and know yourself—knowledge is power)*

17. Don't let big dogs and other guerrillas know too early that you're willing to make concessions. This immediately raises their expectations. If you must tell them, it's much better to reveal this this later on in your

deal-making session, as late as possible. *(Assertive 23, When to speak, when to pause)*

18. Don't accept any of his concessions too soon. If you accept the other guy's offer too quickly without any haggling, he'll start thinking he gave you too much, and he'll try to get out of the deal. *(Assertive 24, Avoid buyer's remorse—don't accept TOS's offer too quickly)*

Words:

19. Don't be afraid to say *no*. In fact, the more you say it, the easier it gets for you. *(Assertive 71, Be stubborn—say no)*

20. Don't say *"I'll think about it"* too often or too easily. Those four words are actually a concession, because they raise his expectations. Watch them drool--both big dogs and other guerrillas! Once again, don't give away any concession without getting one in return. Say instead, "What will you do for me if I even *decide* to think about it." But only if you have more power than the other guy does. *(Defensive 14, Keep TOS's expectations low)*

By the way, these 40 guidelines also appear in Don's chapter in Jay's *Guerrilla Marketing Remix* (Entrepreneur Press, 2011). They are on pages 173-178, Chapter 18, *Guerrilla Deal-Making*.

Following some of these guidelines in Preparation Weapon 19 will be easy for you because you'll readily agree with them. You may resist following others, especially those you have never heard of before, because what you've done in the past has worked for you. But keep an open mind. Try out new things. These 40 guidelines were developed over a long period of time by Don and his clients all over the world. They have used them with great success.

Conclusion

In this chapter you learned many important things, including these:

- How important it is to keep careful records of your concessions and the big dog's concessions.
- How to recognize concession patterns—not only his but yours.
- How to put a dollar value on each concession you both make.
- The 20 do's and 20 don'ts of concession-making.

You're almost finished with your book. You've already read all the tactical Weapons that will make you a winner when you make deals with big dogs and other guerrillas. But before you begin your great adventure armed with Don's 365 Weapons, there's just one more chapter. It tells you how to become so skilled at guerrilla deal-making that you make the right moves *instinctively*. It talks about Don's *Negotiation Poker* game, and gives you the best of Jay Conrad Levinson—his 54 golden rules for guerrilla marketing excellence.

Ready? Go ahead and turn the page.

PART SIX

WRAPPING IT UP

CHAPTER 18

HOW TO BECOME THE ULTIMATE GUERRILLA

What this chapter is all about: From unconsciously unskillful to unconsciously skillful in four steps. Negotiation Poker. How guerrilla deal-makers can use Jay's 54 golden rules for Guerrilla Marketing Excellence.

Introduction: Become the Ultimate Guerrilla by Becoming Unconsciously Skillful at Making Deals

Well, unless you skipped ahead to this chapter, you've finished reading most of your book. So what do you think? How much time will it take for you to master the 100 most powerful Weapons—or even *all* of Don's 365 mainstream Weapons, the Leap Year tactic, and Mao's 22 guerrilla Weapons you saw in Chapter Four? Think about a skill you excel at—perhaps bowling, golf, home repair, juggling, foreign languages, even driving a car. How long did it take you master it? Even if you're talented and have an aptitude for that kind of skill, it probably took you longer than you wanted it to take. That's because you have to go through four stages to become so skillful at something that you do it automatically, without thinking, unconsciously. The four stages are:

- Unconsciously unskillful.
- Consciously unskillful.

- Consciously skillful.
- Unconsciously skillful—the *ultimate guerrilla.*

Stage One: Unconsciously Unskillful. You're so naïve, you don't even know what you don't know—heck you don't even *suspect* anything. You don't even know the right questions to ask. You make the wrong assumptions. For example, the first time an American goes to Australia, he's surprised that light switches turn on downward, not upward like in the U.S. And nobody there will tell you—they take for granted that you're *supposed* to know these things, since everybody else knows them! They don't know you're just plain unconscious. They may even think you're just plain stupid.

Stage Two: Consciously Unskillful. You become aware of what you don't know, and you start asking the right questions. This happened to you when you first opened your book and started to read the fractured fairy tale about Mao Tse-Tung and Donald Trump negotiating with each other. You quickly moved to Stage Two of your skill development process while you read Chapter One. In Stage Two, you stop making so many bad assumptions. And perhaps you begin to worry a little that your ego will soon be deflated.

Stage Three: Consciously Skillful. After a few weeks of practice, you're now semi-skilled. You don't do the right thing automatically. Instead, you have to think about what you should do each time. What you do turns out well most of the time. But you feel frustrated because it's taking longer than you thought it would to become a master your skill. Getting to the next stage may take you a long, long time, depending on how much more you practice. Remember, high speed and skills don't go together.

Stage Four: Unconsciously Skillful. Eventually, you become so skilled, you know what to do subconsciously, you do it automatically, without thinking, and it turns out great almost all the time. You become the *ultimate guerrilla* (Preparation 31). Another Sam Walton. You do things so well, people won't know you did anything at all—and yet you win big, big, big! But a danger often appears now—your ego gets bigger, and this often makes you too arrogant. You start using Assertive Weapons 38 (act arrogant) and 39 (act egotistical) more often. Even though you're now *one with the universe*, you begin to wonder why so many people are so dumb, they don't even know the right questions to ask. Watch out! This kind of attitude may put you on a very slippery slope, and you'll be nothing more than a mediocre deal-maker.

How to Get to Stage Four Quickly—11 Important Hints

These hints are easy to follow, and they really get you on the right track quickly. They are:

- Don't be over-anxious. Realize that becoming unconsciously skillful at anything, including deal-making, will take much longer than you think it will.
- Be committed to your goal of becoming unconsciously skillful at winning deals with the big dog.
- Try to use as many of the 100 most powerful Weapons—and the other 265 Weapons—as often as possible. And the more than 400 Counter-punches in your book. Take notes. Which ones work best for you? Which ones work best for the big dog?
- Remember that each Weapon works in certain situations. In some other situations, though, it won't work. You'll eventually learn when to use a given Weapon—and when *not* to.
- Continue to use the Weapons that work best for you.
- Practice deal-making as often as you can. With your spouse. With hard-sell car dealers. With total strangers—try your elevator speech on them.
- You'll often be in situations that aren't too important to you. Such as buying furniture at a used furniture store. Or browsing at a garage sale. In those kinds of situations, think of deal-making as a game. Haggle to your heart's content. Weapons that work for you consistently at these kinds of places will probably work for you in more important situations, such as getting a raise from your boss.
- Eventually, think of *all* deal-making as a game. It will be less stressful for you that way.
- How do you know if you've won the game or not? Money. A wise multi-millionaire, Paul Young, once told Don, "The money's not that important. It's just how you keep score."
- So keep score. Try out some of Don's 365 Weapons. And the several hundred Counter-punches. Find out *which* ones work and don't work. And *when* they work and when they don't work. And *why* they work and why they don't work.

- A good way to find out which Weapons work, go to **www. DonaldHendon.com/NegotiationPoker**, and play Don's *Negotiation Poker*© game a few times. Then, try the complete version. It's available at **www.GuerrillaDon.com**. Apps for iPhones, iPads, iPods, and Androids are also available there—also DVDs and CD-ROMs.

The 12th Way: Use the Prism of Power

A 12th way to get to Stage Four quickly is to look at the *Prism of Power*, which we talked about briefly in Chapter Six. The Prism has 95 guidelines, and it's in Don's *365 Powerful Ways to Influence* book. Do things that give you more power and avoid things that take away your power. Mastering the prism is easier than you think. Even though it has 122 guidelines, it contains only 744 words. Or you can check out Don's Prism of Power at **www.GuerrillaDon.com**. Don's website has more details than his book does.

To help you get started on your journey to becoming unconsciously skillful, here's a good roadmap to follow—the best of Jay Conrad Levinson—54 Golden Rules to follow. It's a 1,700-word summary of his book, *Guerrilla Marketing Excellence—Golden Rules for Small-Business Success*.

54 Golden Rules for Guerrillas

Jay's 54 golden rules are in 33 categories:

Attention to your customers
1. Your marketing has an obligation to capture the attention and hold the interest of as many prospects as possible—big dogs and guerrillas alike.
2. Get their attention quickly: If you have ten hours to spend creating an ad, spend nine of them on the headline.

Attention to details
3. Don't neglect details : Your marketing will succeed only if sufficient time and energy are regularly devoted to it by you or a trusted person you delegate this task to.

Believability

4. Create a path of least resistance to the sale. How? By paving the path with credibility.

Benefits or solutions?
5. It's a lot easier to sell a solution to a problem than to sell a positive benefit.

Bonding
6. Create a bond by adding a touch of humanity: Remember, everyone you market to is a human being first and a customer next.

Your bottom line
7. Keep a close watch on your bottom line: The key to marketing economically isn't in saving money—it's by making every investment pay off handsomely.

The guerrilla calendar, thinking ahead, and timing
8. The guerrilla calendar: When planning and producing marketing and then evaluating it, use Jay's guerrilla calendar idea. This means don't be in a hurry—take your time. Doing things in a hurry costs too much, and you tend to overlook things.
9. The guerrilla calendar: Don't think of sales transactions as single events. Think of them as starts or continuations of close and lasting relationships.
10. Think ahead: When you're blessed with the guerrilla's vision, you won't seek instant gratification. You'll find your rewards with your farsightedness.
11. Timing: The right marketing to the right people is only right when your timing is right.

Control
12. If you don't take control of your marketing, your company's future will be in the hands of your competitors. In other words, *Eat life, or life will eat you.*

Cooperate, don't compete

13. To assure your marketing success, you're got to become more oriented to cooperation than competition.

Your customers

14. Customer or opponent?: If you think of the person you're trying to make a deal with as your customer, not as your opponent, you'll probably win more.

15. Know your customers. The ability to accurately define your precise market dramatically affects your profitability.

16. Care for your customers. To be successful, you have to care for your customers—don't just pay attention to them. More companies fail than succeed, and the ones that succeed are the ones that prove to customers that they care about them.

17. Make sure your customers know how much you care about them. Consistently display your reverence for your customers by trying to help them with consistent follow-up.

18. Go beyond caring—pamper your most important customers, both big dogs and other guerrillas alike. If you have an especially important customer, market to that person in an especially important way. For example, if your company has a luxury lounge in a sports stadium, invite him to sit with you in several games.

19. Pamper your ordinary customers, too. Design your business to operate for the convenience of your customers. Make it very easy for them to do business with you.

20. Offer them benefits, not features. Gear your marketing to people already in the market, and know what they really buy other than plain old instant gratification. In other words, all you've got to do is consistently put across any one of the many benefits of what you're offering to the people who want them *right now*. When you do this, you've virtually made the sale.

21. Interact with your customers. Questions lead to answers. Answers lead to customer rapport. Customer rapport leads to profits.

22. It's easier to achieve a healthy market share if you first obtain a healthy share of mind. And so if you follow golden rules 14-21, you'll make sure they think of you first when they want something instead of thinking of your competitor.

23. The downside of a healthy share of mind: On the other hand, if you have that healthy share of mind, you may end up taking your customers for granted. Never fall into that trap. It's wise to be first in line when your prospect buys, but it's often more profitable to be second in line. Why? Those who are first in line tend to screw up first, too. Businesses who are first in line tend to do nine things:

- Ignore their customers.
- Give them less-than-caring service.
- Fall short of quality expectations.
- Be late with deliveries.
- Raise prices a little too high.
- Keep callers on hold too long.
- Fail to show up on time for an appointment.
- Be outgunned in the area of convenience.
- Do something to lose the confidence of their customers.

So, customers go to businesses that were second in line.

Get help
24. Let a professional produce your marketing materials, because even a hint of amateurism can lose sales for you.

Gifts and gimmicks
25. Gifts, something extra: Whatever term you use to describe it, the truth remains that everybody loves to be bribed. Especially big dogs.
26. Gimmicks—use them: Despite how solid you're committed to a plan, sometimes a guerrilla's just got to have a gimmick. For example: Hand out two business cards, one to keep, and one with a coupon printed on it for a 25 percent discount on your customer's first order.

Give or take?
27. Companies that think of what they can *give* to people make more profits than companies that think of what they can *take* from people.
Honesty

28. Be honest. Do everything in your power to use marketing techniques and tactics that are honest and beyond reproach.

Humor

29. Humor—be careful when you use it. Avoid using humor unless it's pertinent to your offering and doesn't detract from your offer.

Information and knowledge

30. Value of information: Your own customer list is the best in the world—but only if it bulges with information about each customer. Does it?
31. Your stock-in-trade: The more know-how you have about the overall marketing process, the more profits you'll make.

Networking

32. Be a successful networker. How? Ask questions, listen to answers, and focus on the problems of your networking group.

New offerings—new products and services

33. When introducing your new offerings, enthusiastically announce that they're new, and clearly explain why they're good.

One at a time

34. Tiny shares of gigantic marketing are abundant and profitable if you serve and market to one person at a time.

Originality and uniqueness

35. Originality—no. Don't invest too much money in originality. Remember, your major investment should be in generating profits.
36. Originality—yes. Identify or create your competitive advantages. Use them extensively in your marketing efforts.
37. Occupy a unique niche. Market your services successfully by capitalizing upon the bountiful opportunities to create a unique niche.

Pioneer

38. The perils of being a pioneer: If you're going to pioneer with a new product or service, you must be prepared for walls of apathy and fear.

Profit-oriented

39. Be profit-oriented. Everything in your marketing should be designed to increase your profits. Not your sales numbers, but your profits.

Protect yourself from other guerrillas

40. Maximize your profits by remembering that the best defense is a good offense.

Recessions

41. During recessions, focus your efforts on existing customers and larger transactions.

Restrain yourself

42. Don't be a perfectionist—don't fix it unless you're absolutely positive it's broken.

Sell, don't show off

43. Emphasize the meat and potatoes of your offering, rather than the plate upon which they're served.
44. Marketing is always more effective if it is looked upon as selling rather than show-time.

Be specific

45. The believability and persuasion of your marketing increase in direct proportion to how much specific data you give your customers.

Become a spy

46. Make sure you're better than your competitors by spying on them: The more you spy on your competition, your industry, and yourself, the more opportunities you'll find to improve.

Television and social media—borrow power from them

47. When you're making deals with retailers, remember it's possible to have your product sold in almost any store you choose if you use TV

marketing for leverage. Today, social media seems to be even more powerful.

Un-satisfy them—make them ask for more

48. It's easier to get someone to take the hard step of buying if they first take the softer step of requesting more data from you.

Your Weapons

49. Don't rely on just one marketing Weapon. Many marketing Weapons attain their maximum effectiveness only when you combine them with other marketing Weapons.

Words

50. Clever or pertinent? People will remember the most clever part of your marketing, but make sure it pertains directly to what you are selling.

51. Word Power 1: Make sure you catch your prospect's attention quickly. Prepare. If you have ten hours to spend creating an ad, spend nine of them on the headline.

52. Word Power 2: The right words will propel a great idea toward success. The wrong words will doom a great idea to failure. Here are the 35 most powerful words to use in your ads and sales pitches:

First, here are the four most powerful of all the 35:

- New
- Save
- You
- Your

The rest are alphabetical:
- Advice
- Alternative
- Announcing
- Benefits
- Comfortable
- Discover

- Easy
- Fun
- Gain
- Good-looking
- Guaranteed
- Happy
- Healthy
- Introducing
- Love
- Money
- Now
- People
- Proud
- Proven
- Results
- Right
- Safe
- Sale
- Security
- Trustworthy
- Value
- Wanted
- Why
- Win
- Winnings

And don't use these 17 words—too negative:
- Bad
- Buy
- Cost
- Contract
- Death
- Decision
- Difficult
- Fail
- Failure

- Hard
- Liability
- Loss
- Obligation
- Order
- Sell
- Worry
- Wrong

Are these rules made to be broken?

53. Don't be afraid to break these 52 golden rules. But break them only if you have a good reason. And make sure you *know* you're breaking a rule when you do it. At least you'll be acting with a purpose, rather than with ignorance. Remember, it's a waste of your money to break a rule by accident.

54. Come up with your own golden rules. Don't be afraid to experiment. Guerrilla marketing encourages experimentation, even at the risk of failed experiments. Don't let cold feet keep you from potentially hot ideas. Use whatever works best for you, and discard whatever doesn't work.

Conclusion

We hope you become bigger winners than you are now. We *know* you will if you master what you've read in your book. Combine what you've learned here with your God-given talent. The unconventional Weapons we've given you in this book of yours will help you get what you want from others most of the time. We've seen guerrillas use them with great success. And we've even seen a few big dogs who think outside the box use them to get what they want from guerrillas. Good luck!

But Before You Close the Book Cover…

We hope you contact us. Please send us your questions, your problems, and your suggestions for improving this book you have just finished reading. Become a part of the next book in this series by Don and Jay—*More Guerrilla Deal-Making: Winning Ideas from Successful Guerrillas*. We'll try to include as many ideas as possible from you in our next editions and in other books we write. Here's more about us and how to get in touch with us:

Jay Conrad Levinson

I have been so successful because I have been thinking outside the box ever since I began my marketing career. I was the first to use the term *Guerrilla Marketing* to describe unconventional marketing tools for organizations to use when they have limited resources. Wikipedia says *Guerrilla Marketing* is the best known marketing brand in history. It was named one of the 100 best business books ever written, with over 28 million copies sold. My guerrilla concepts have influenced marketing so much that my books appear in 62 languages and are required reading in MBA programs worldwide. I have worked with giant ad agencies, including Leo Burnett and J. Walter Thompson. I developed marketing campaigns for many well-known brands, including the Marlboro Man, the Pillsbury Doughboy, Tony the Tiger, the Jolly Green Giant, Allstate Insurance's *Good Hands*, United Airlines' *Friendly Skies*, and Sears' Diehard Battery.

And of course, I am widely-known as the Father of Guerrilla Marketing. I'm famous throughout the world. Google me. You'll find millions of hits. (When you google Donald Hendon, you'll get millions of hits, too!)

Contact me by going to my website, **www.gmarketing.com**.

Donald Wayne Hendon

The most unique information I have to share with my clients: Specific negotiation tactics—those most favored by executives from more than 60 nations. Advance knowledge of these Weapons prepares executives when they negotiate with people from these nations—and gives them the power to win more. You'll see a small sample of these specific Weapons in Chapter Two, pages 27-28.

Where did I get this information? I have given in-house and public seminars and done consulting in 36 nations on six continents where I have interacted with and coached over 60 nationalities. I'll be glad to send you a list of 100 of my major clients. Some of them are: McDonald's, Coca-Cola, Nissan, Johnson & Johnson, the Las Vegas Convention and Visitors Authority, Australian Association of National Advertisers, Association of Canadian Advertisers, Philippine Airlines, and, once upon a time, Jimmy Carter's peanut business. And here are some of my seminar offerings:

- Negotiating-persuasion-influence-power
- International negotiating
- Body language
- Marketing warfare, guerrilla marketing, marketing strategy dumb marketing mistakes
- Management skills and tools
- Creativity and entrepreneurship
- Customer relations, service, salesmanship, sales management

I have written six other books, published in 14 nations, ten languages, along with several hundred other publications. Books: *365 Powerful Ways to Influence, Battling for Profits, How to Negotiate Worldwide, Cross-Cultural Business Negotiations, Classic Failures in Product Marketing, American Advertising*. And several hundred articles in many different trade journals and academic journals.

University teaching career: I have had over 30 years full-time teaching, various universities in U.S. (13 states and Puerto Rico) and abroad (Australia, Canada, Mexico, Malaysia, Oman, Saudi Arabia, United Arab Emirates). 13 states: Texas, Arkansas, Louisiana, Alabama, Georgia, Tennessee, Florida, Nebraska, South Dakota, Wyoming, Utah, Nevada, Hawaii. I retired from full-time teaching in 2002 to devote myself to consulting, coaching, training, seminars, and writing books.

My degrees: Ph.D. from the University of Texas at Austin (1971). MBA from the University of California at Berkeley (1964). BBA from The University of Texas at Austin (1962).

E-mail: donhendon1@aol.com

Postal address: P. O. Box 2624, Mesquite, Nevada 89024, USA. Mesquite is 80 miles from Las Vegas.

Websites: **www.GuerrillaDon.com** and **www.DonaldHendon.com**. Click on **GuerrillaDon** to get more information about many subjects in your book.

We'd like to close your book with a traditional Irish friendship wish from both of us:

May there always be work for your hands to do.
May your purse always hold a coin or two.
May the sun always shine on your windowpane.

May a rainbow be certain to follow each rain.
May the hand of a friend always be near you.
May God fill your heart with gladness to cheer you.

GET YOUR FREE GIFT!

As Promised on the Front Cover...

Bonus—Get a free Guerrilla Deal-Making Secrets Kit...

a $97 value

Highlights from the best of Donald Wayne Hendon's seminars

Learn practical and powerful ideas that are
guaranteed to ***transform*** your career

You'll get highlights from these 10 seminars:

- The prism of power—how to get others to do what you want them to do
- Winning entrepreneurship—how to start your own business and make lots of money
- How to improve your efficiency at work and at home
- How to deal with difficult people—good conflict and bad conflict
- How to set and achieve your lifetime goals
- How to get ahead in your career—quickly
- Time mastery—finally, the best way to manage your time
- Battling for profits—how to win in marketing warfare
- How to be more creative
- How to make decisions and solve problems without ulcers

 To get these 10 highlights free right now, go to:
www.GuerrillaDon.com/FreeHighlights